Grimm's Fairy Tales

Adult Coloring Book

Life is full of things that stress us out. Between work, children, bills, and chores at home, our minds are inundated with stuff vying for our attention. Coloring is a great way to relax and allow stress to melt away.

Have a problem you are trying to figure out? Just open up this book, take your colored pencils, and begin filling in the blank spaces. Don't focus on anything, but coloring what is within this book. By doing this, you will clear your mind, and just might come up with the solution you've been searching for.

With 30 designs to color, this book has something for every skill level. So just take a moment to relax and color.

You can tear this page out and use it to put between the images so as to avoid bleed through.

The Frog Prince

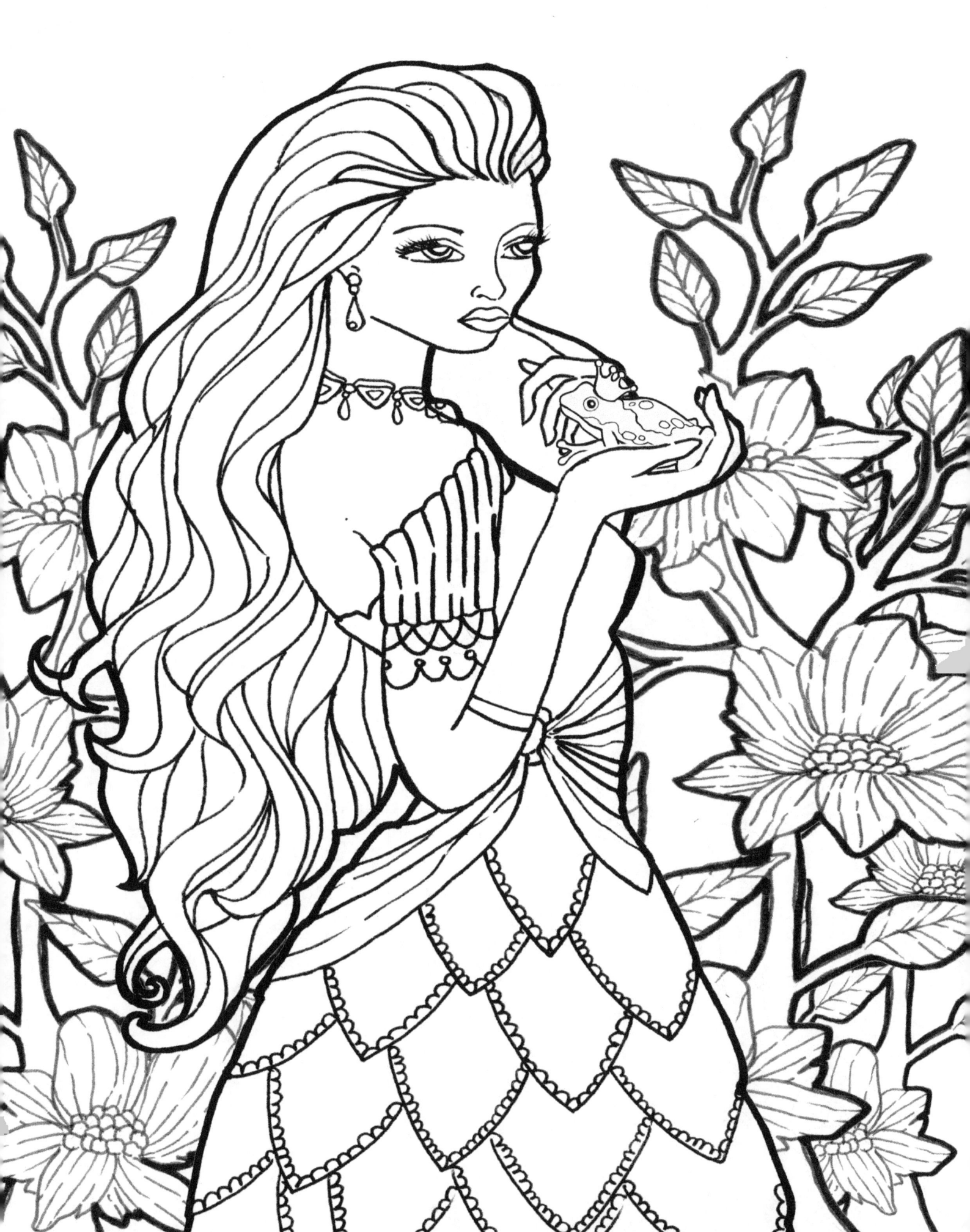

Hansel and Gretel

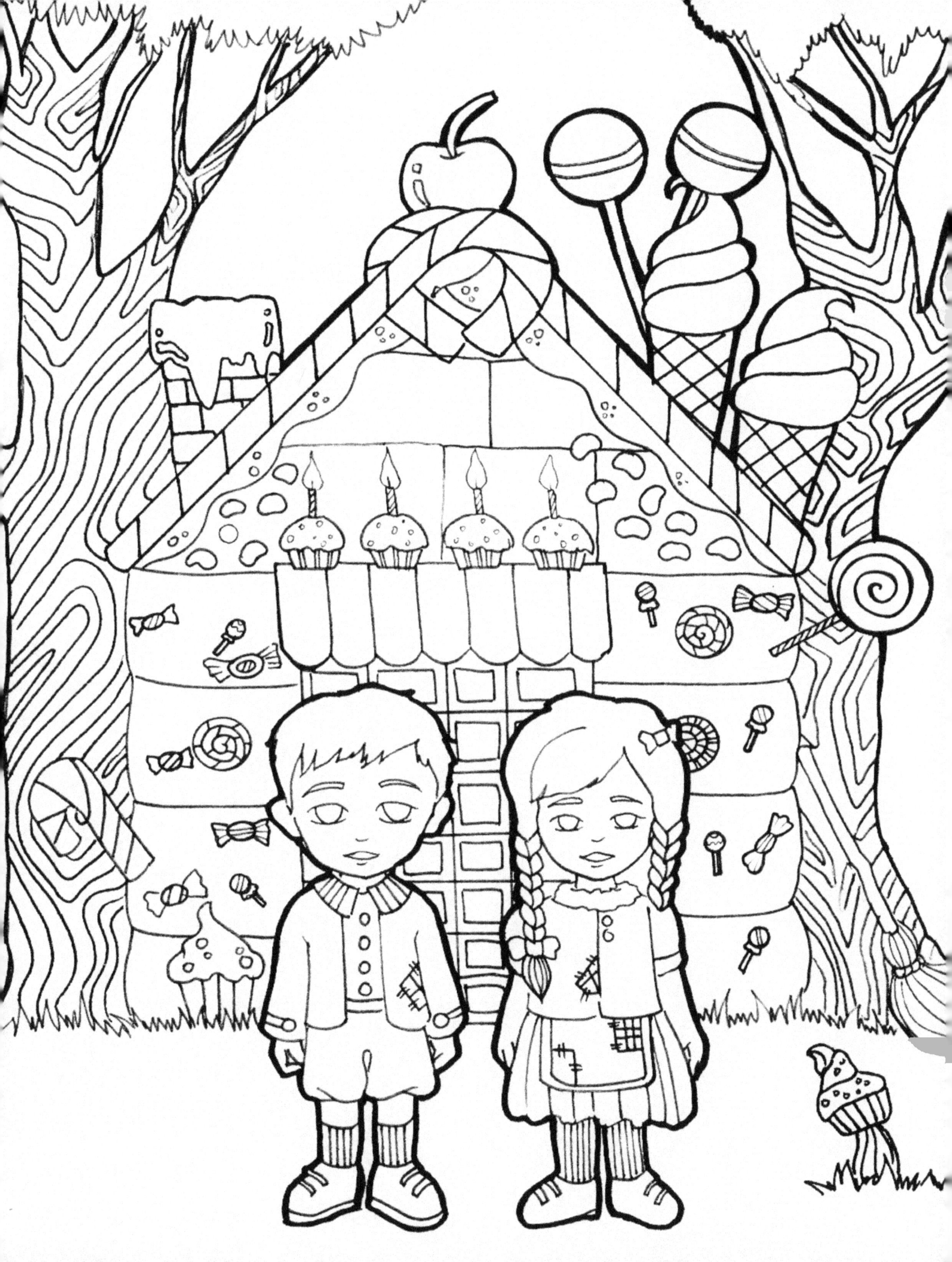

Rapunzel

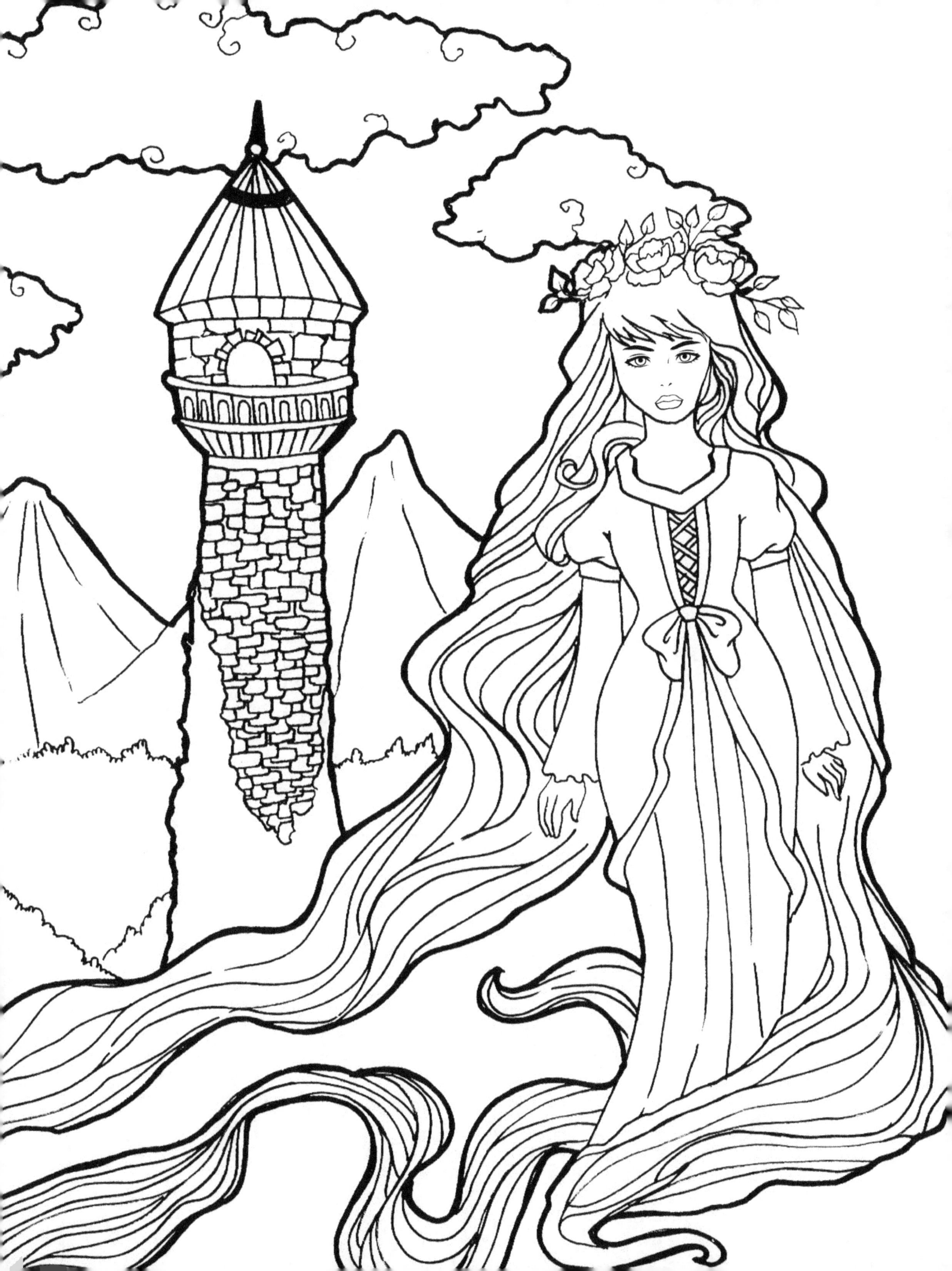

The Fisherman's Wife

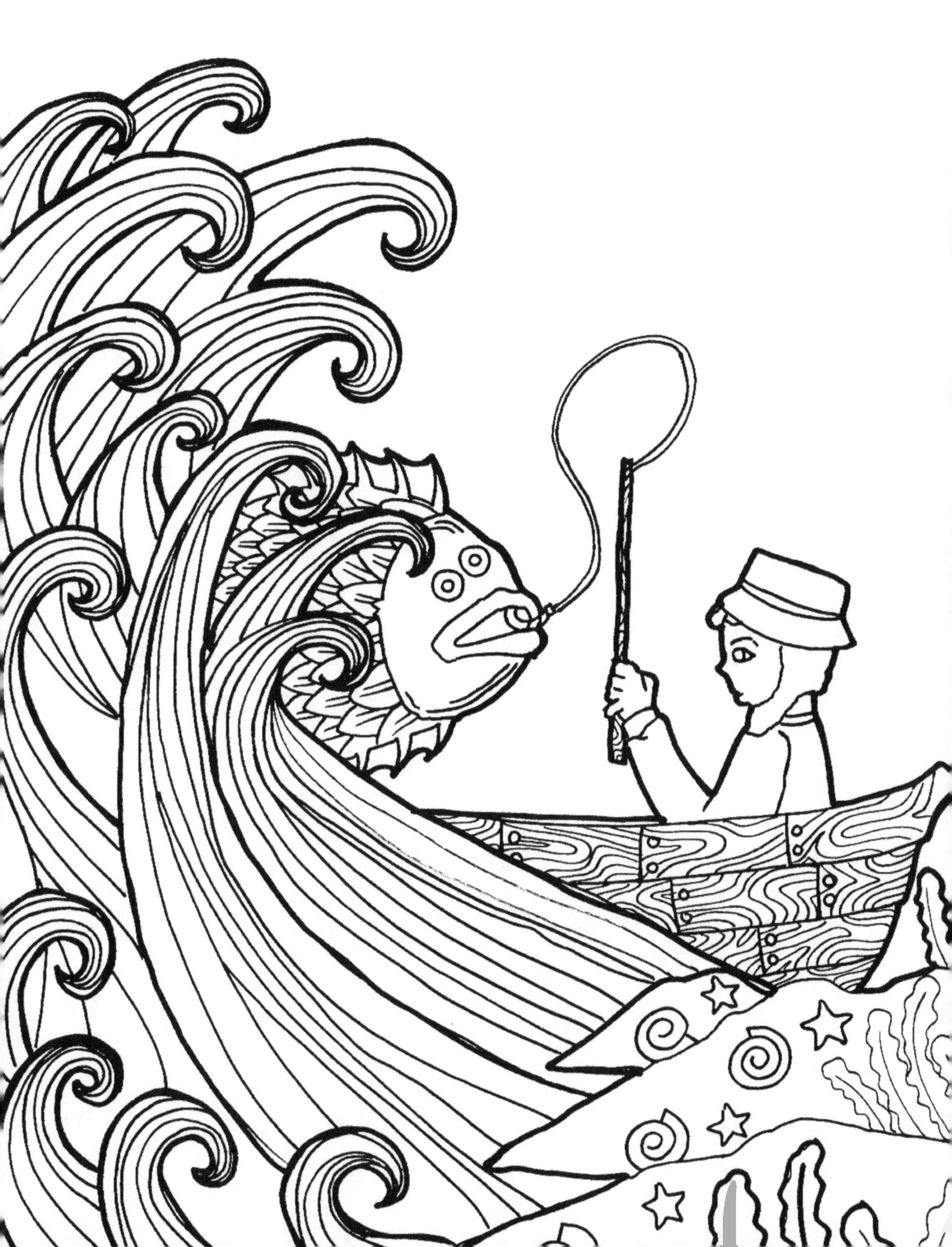

Cinderella

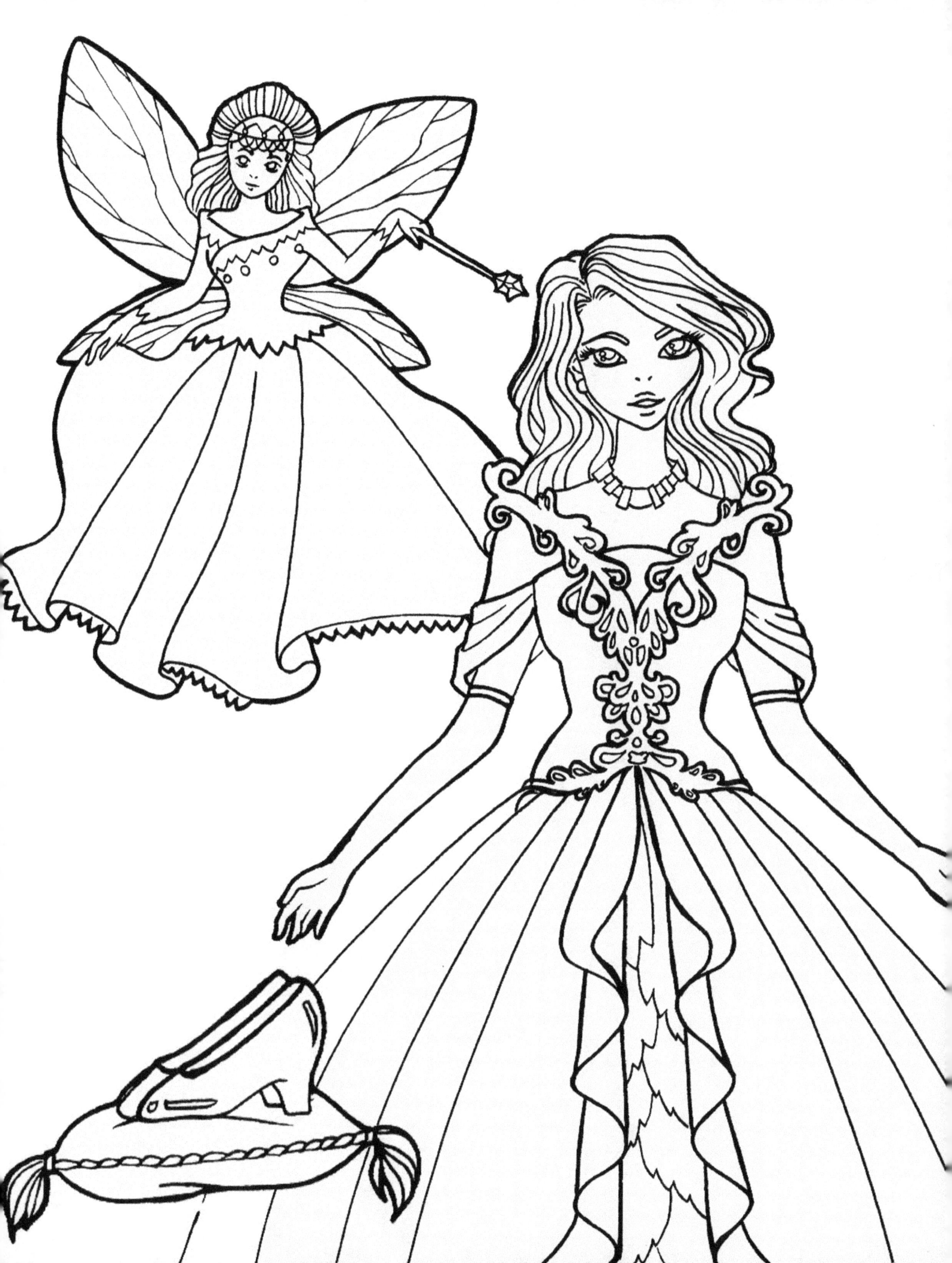

Mother Holle

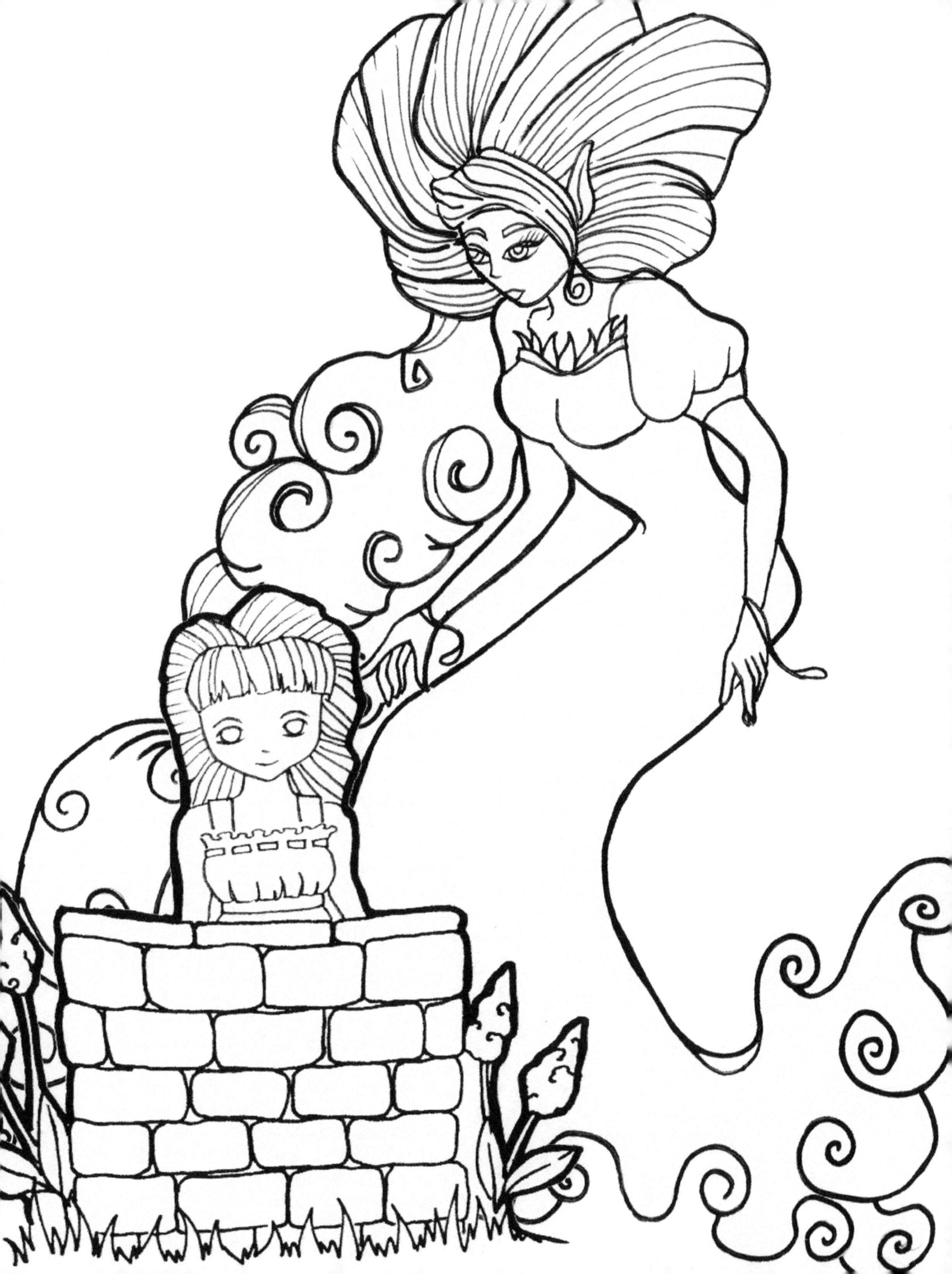

The Two Brothers

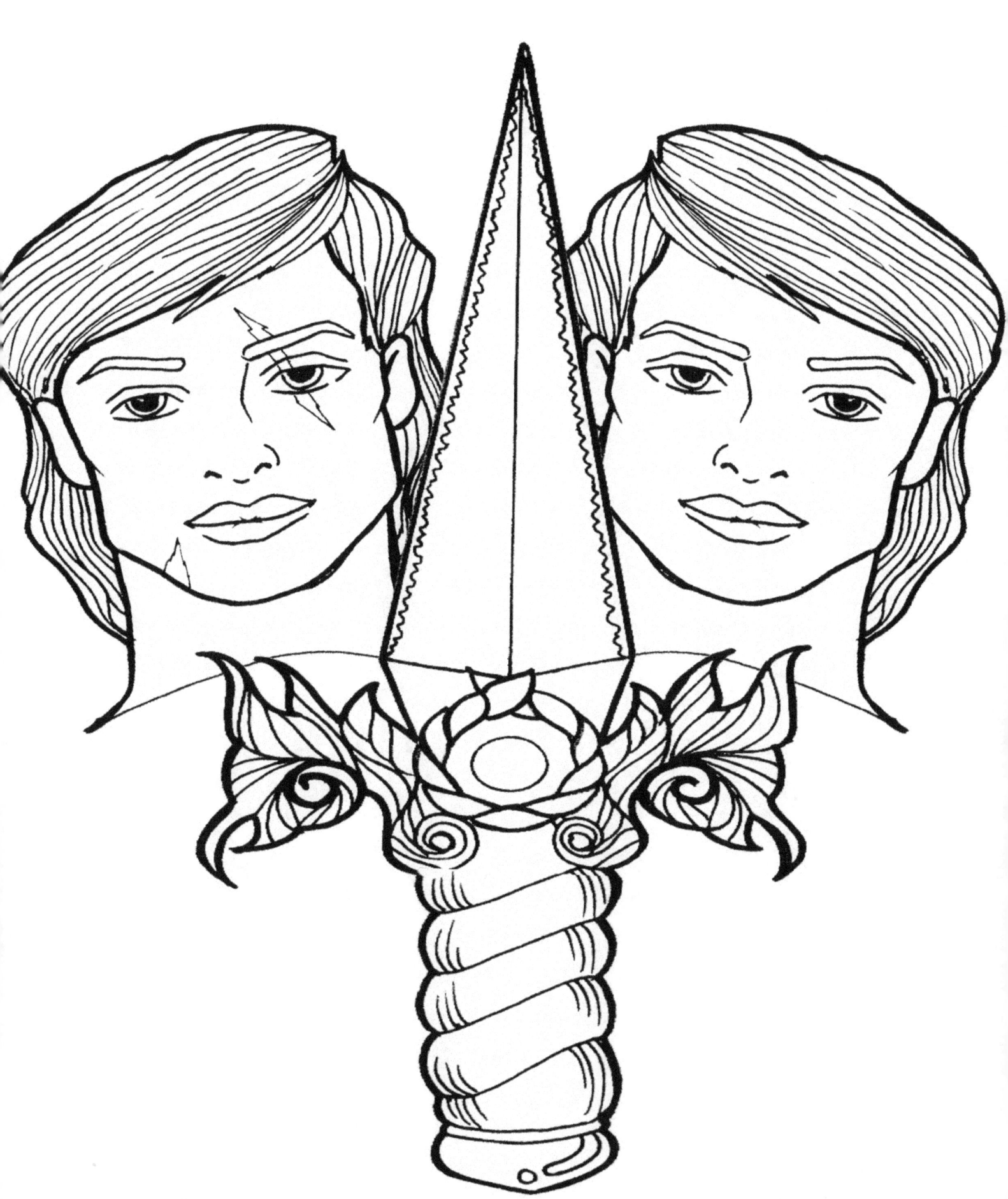

The Seven Ravens

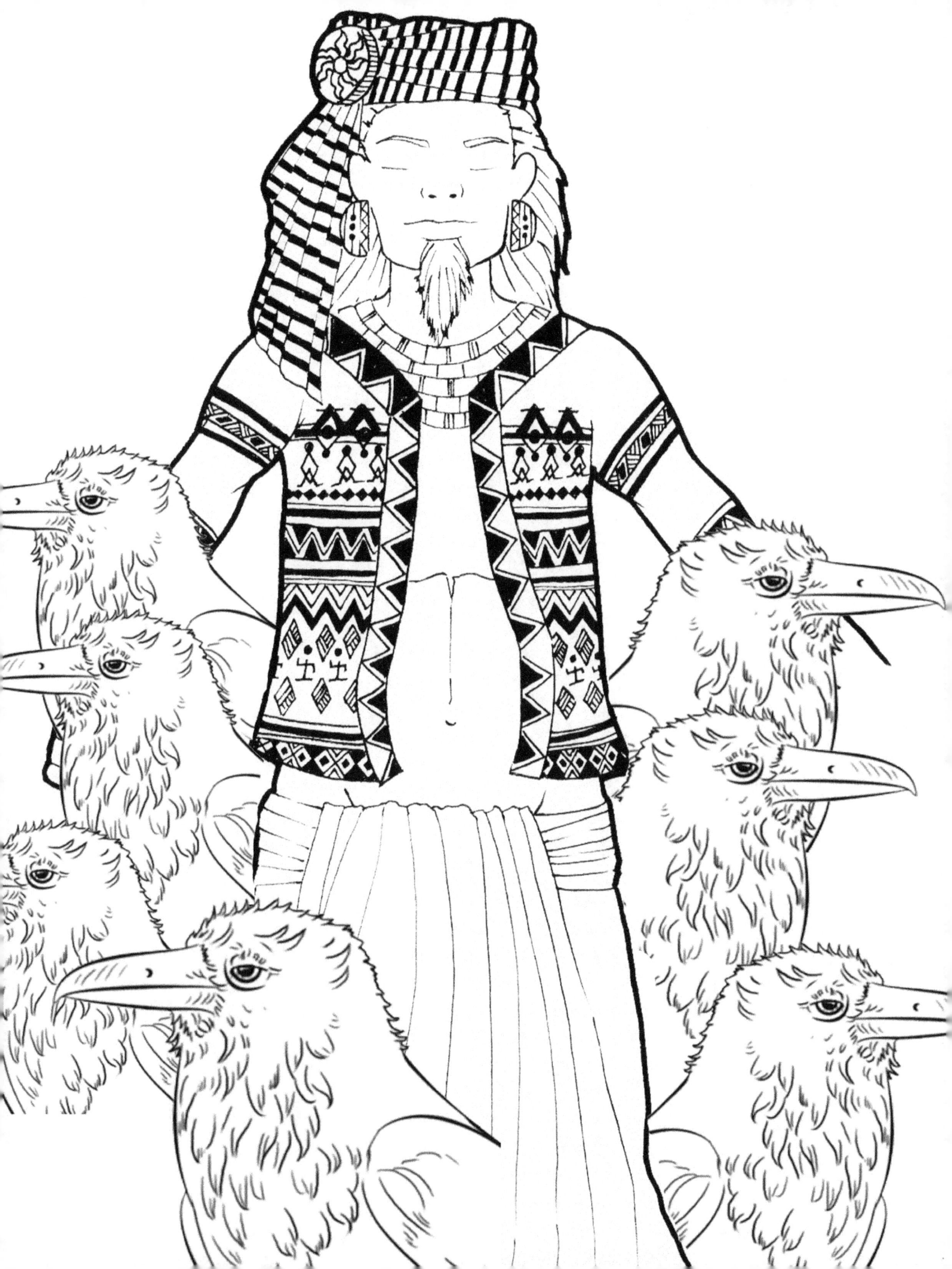

The Twelve Brothers

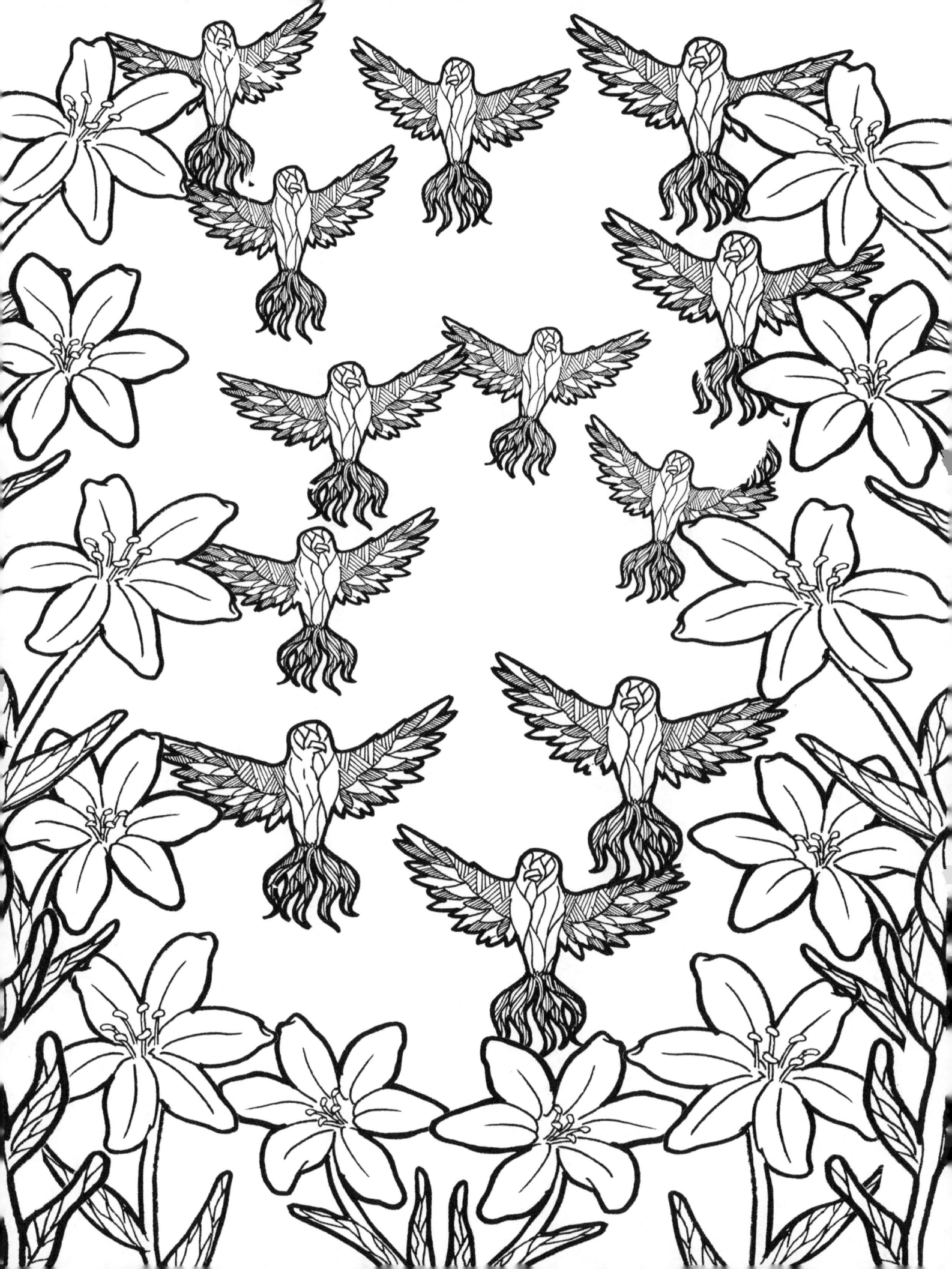

Little Red Cap

AKA
Little Red Riding Hood

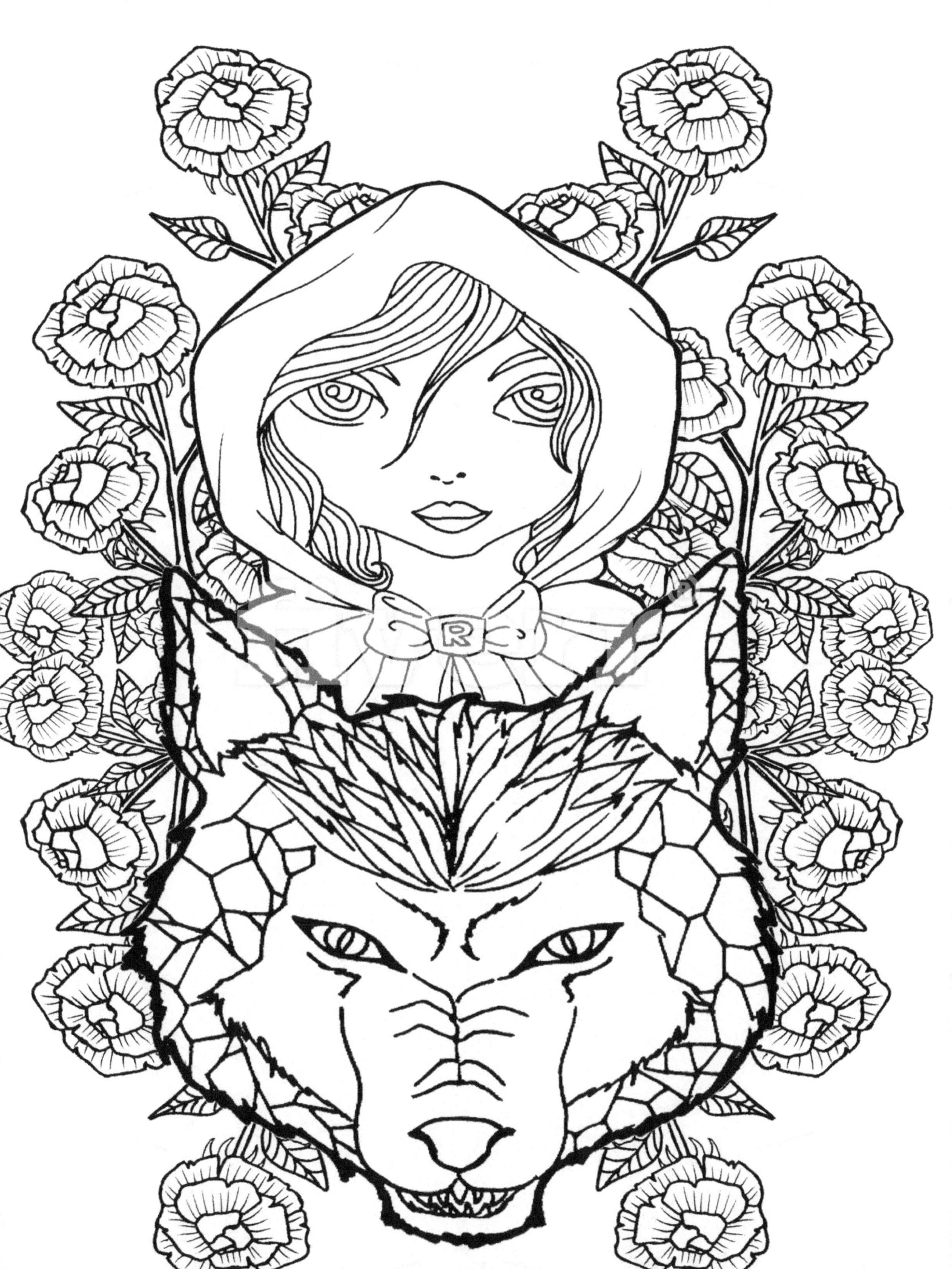

The Devil with Three Golden Hairs

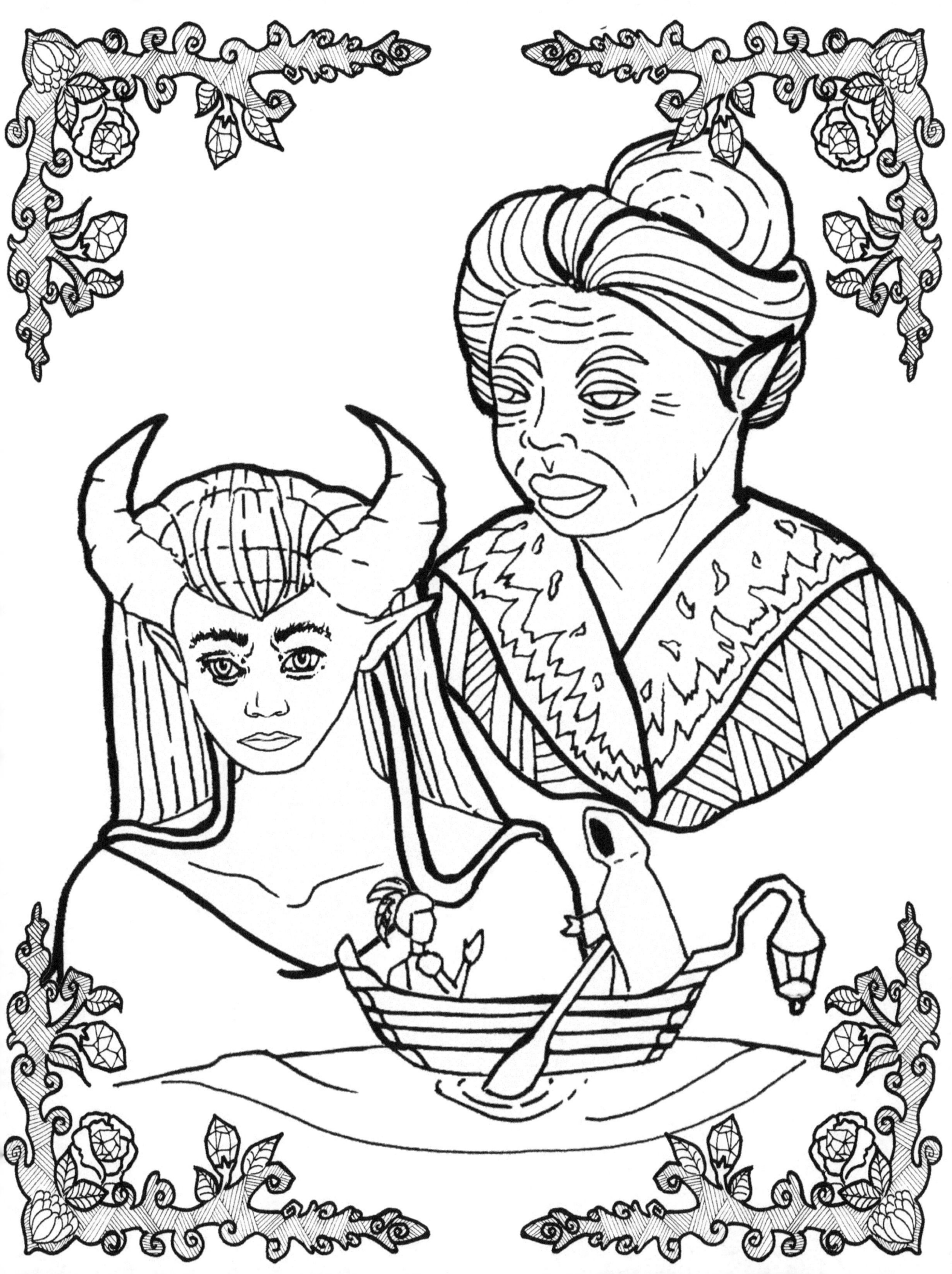

The Three
Leaves Snake

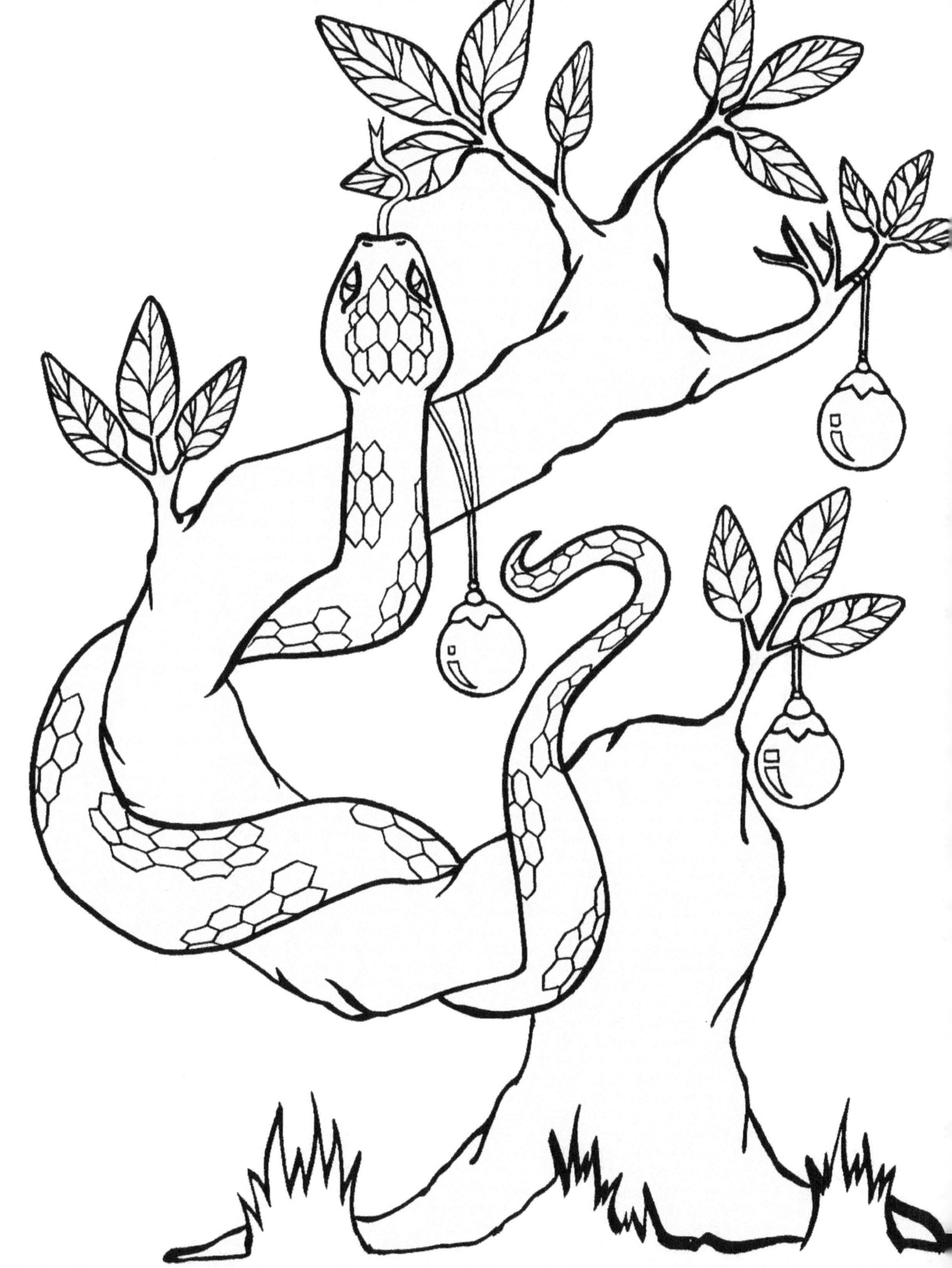

The Riddle

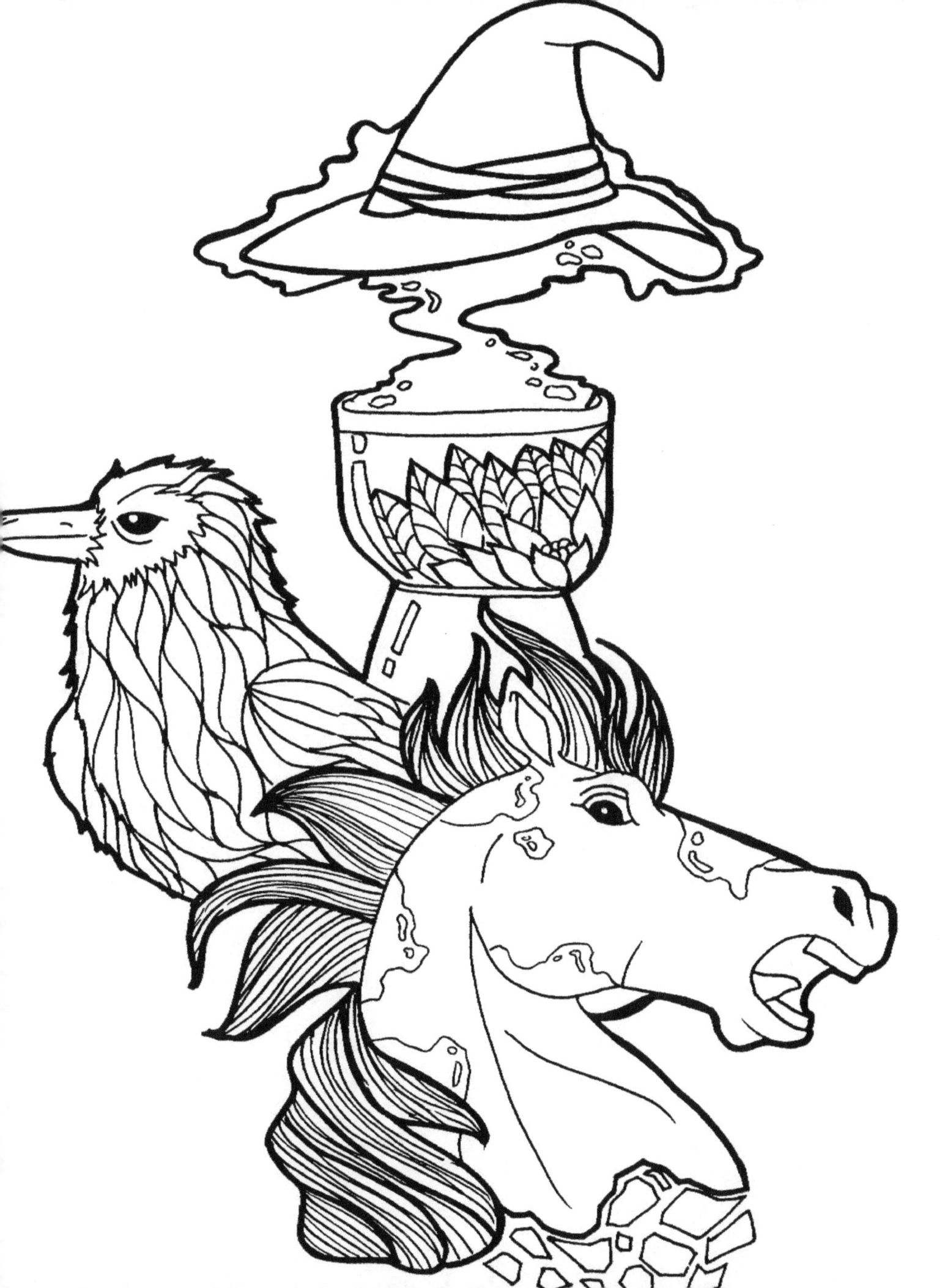

Thumbling

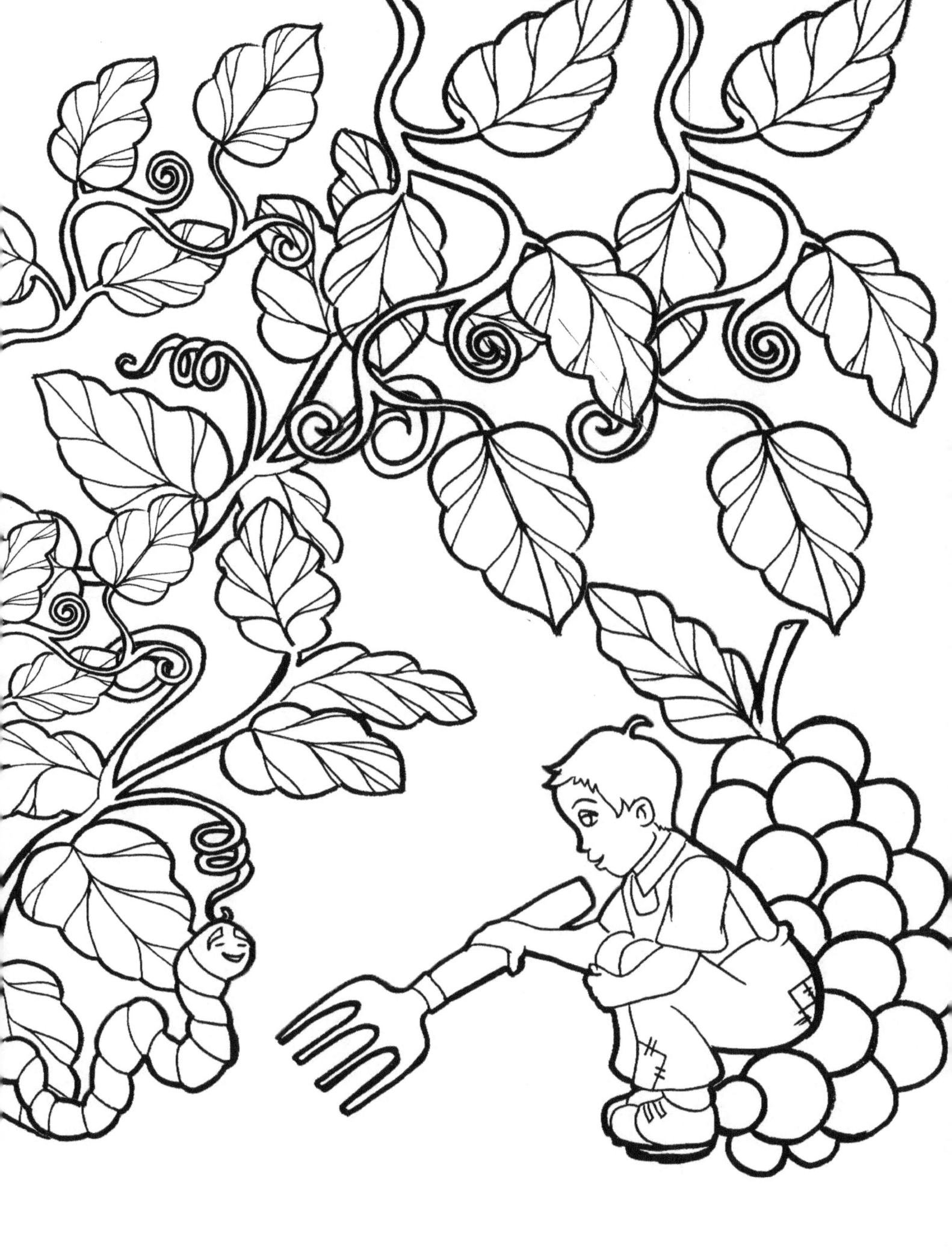

The Elves

AKA
The Elves and the Shoemaker

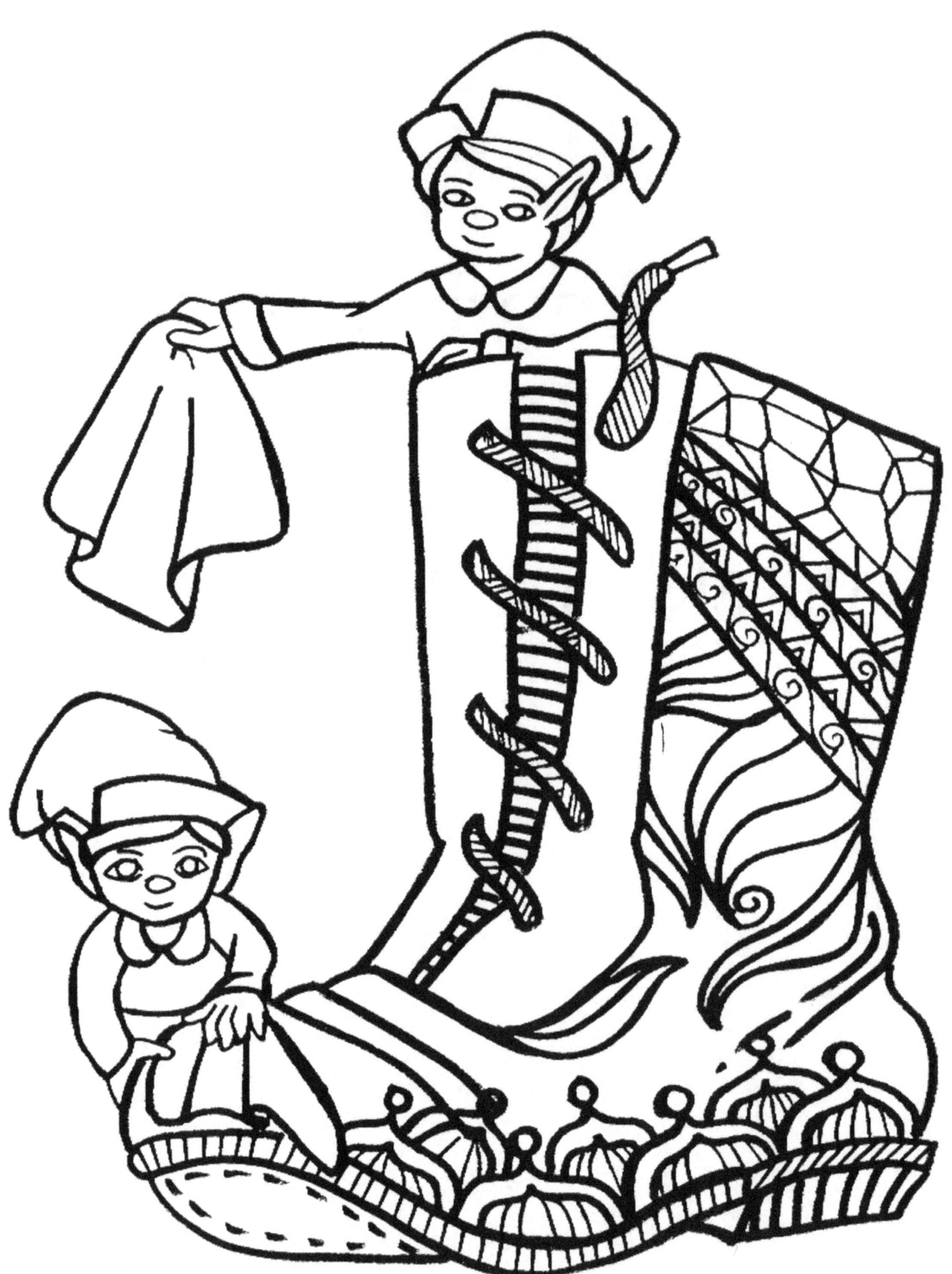

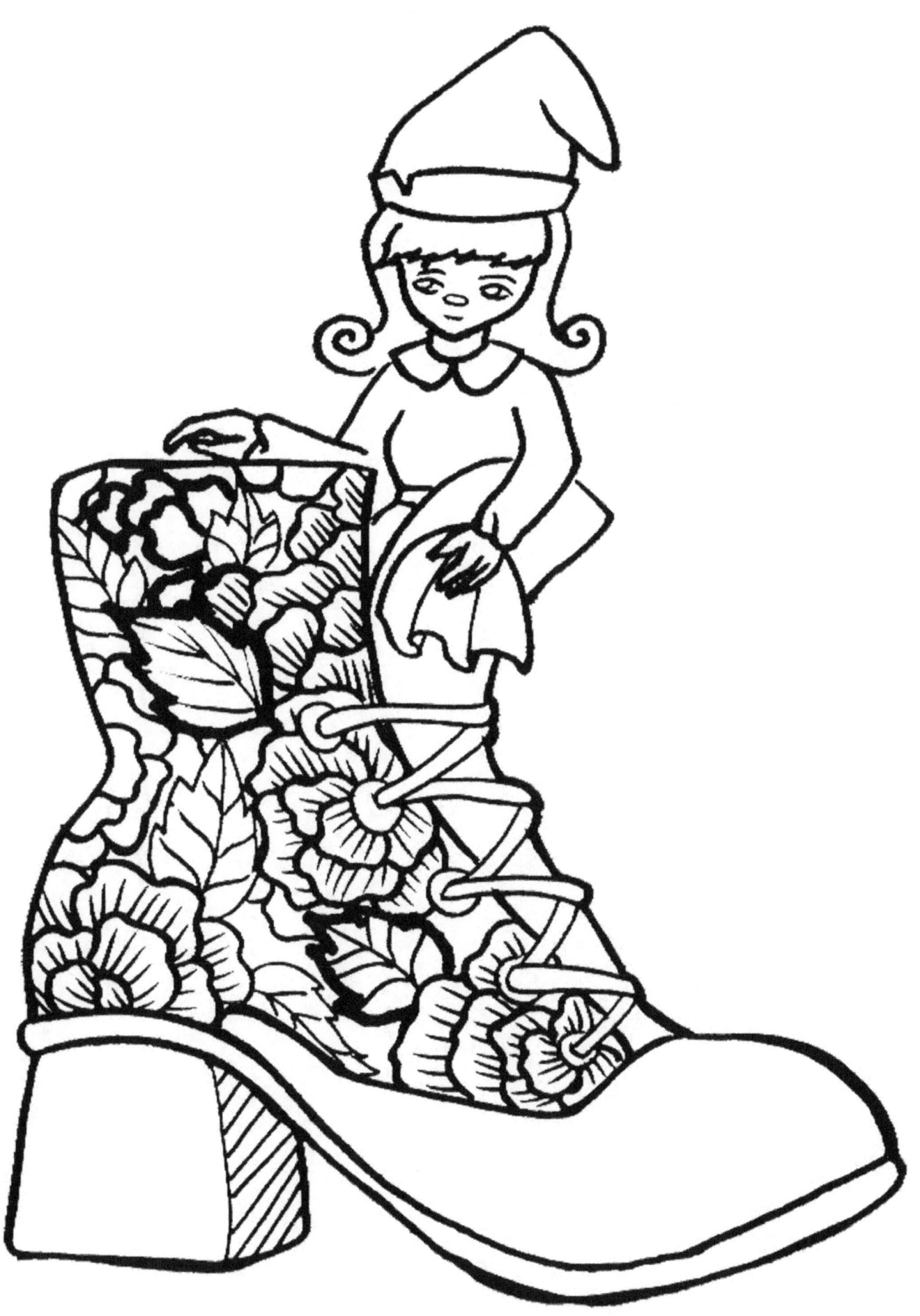

The Singing Bone

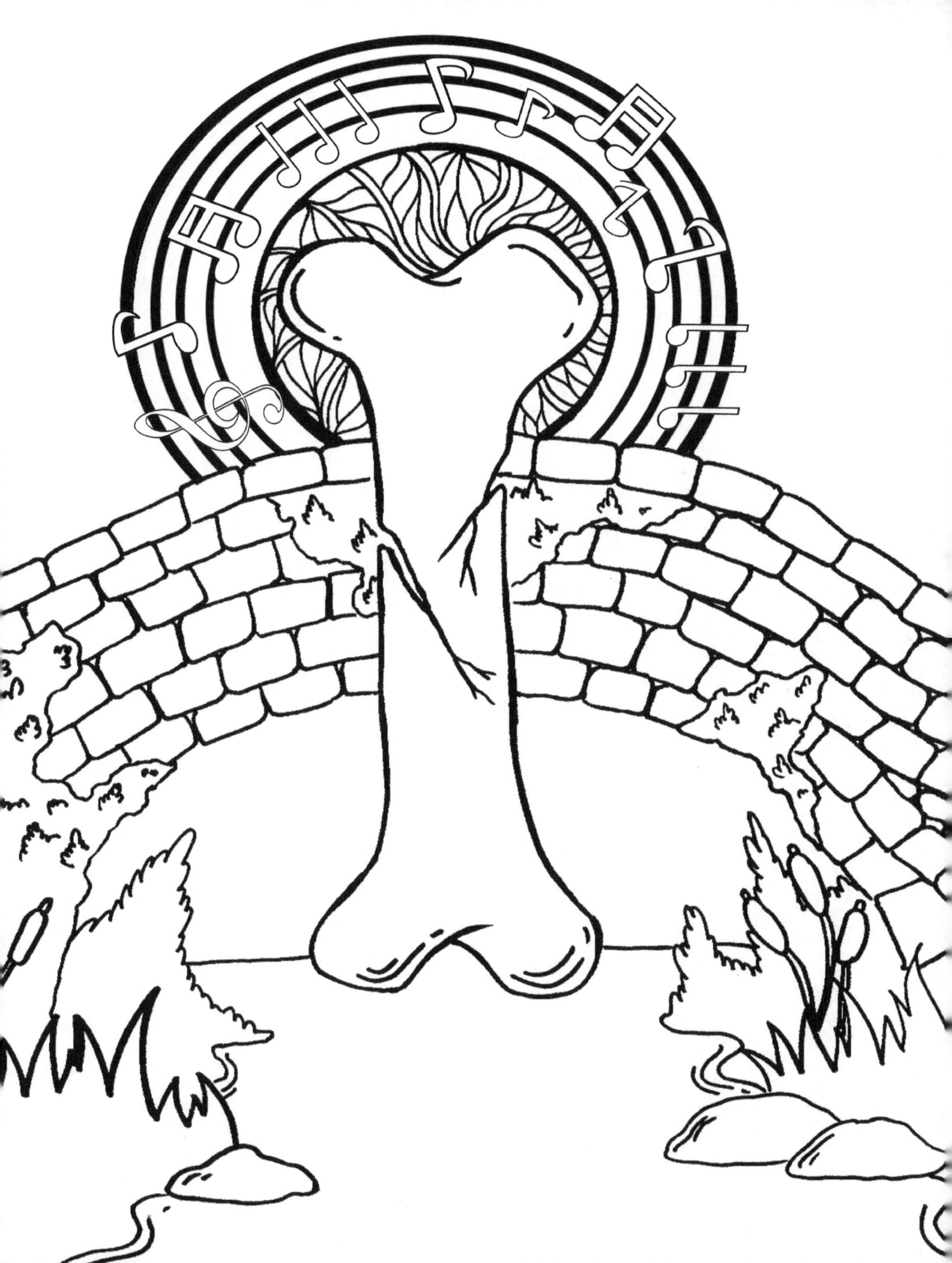

The Six Swans

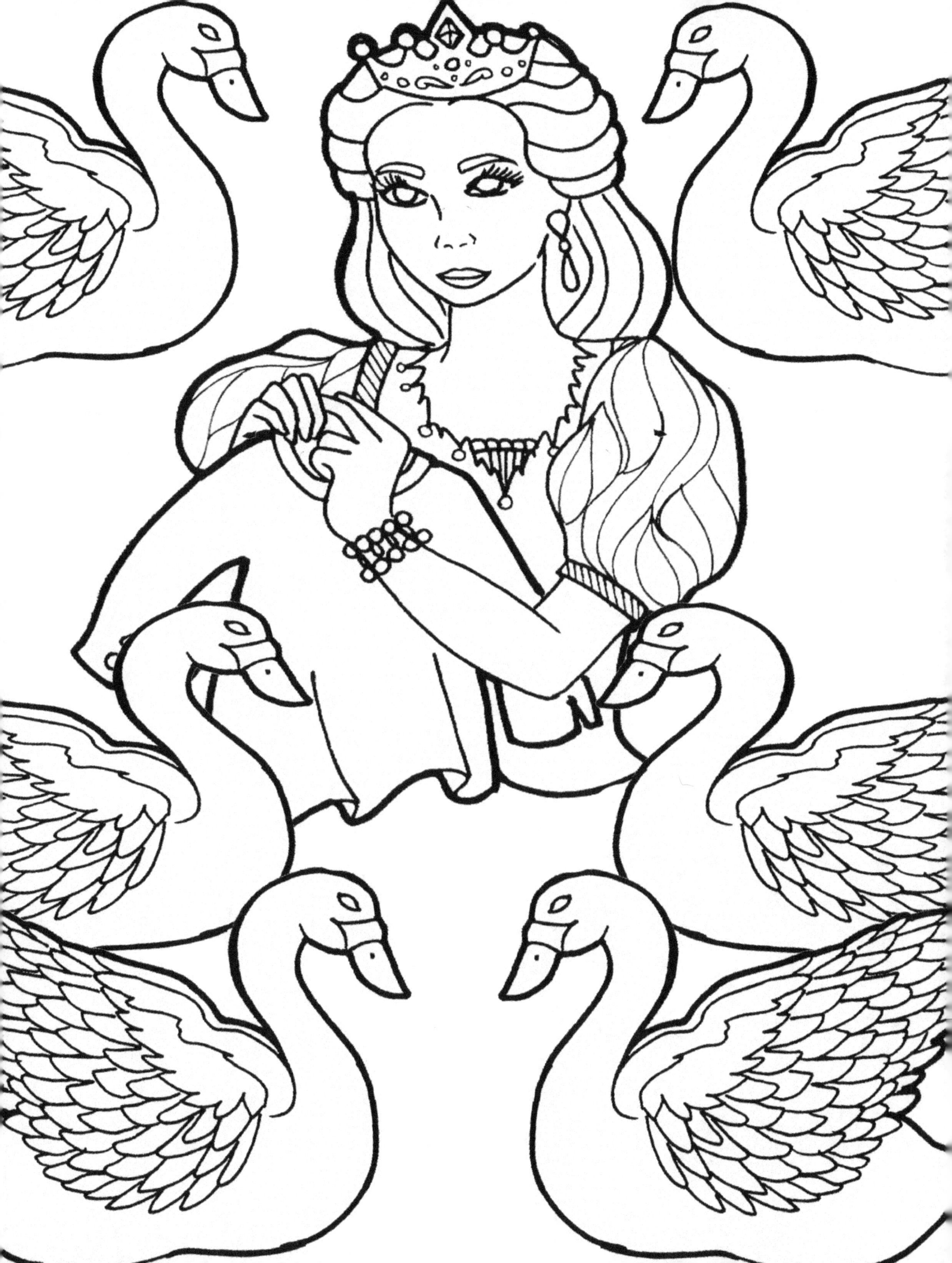

Little Briar Rose

AKA
Sleeping Beauty

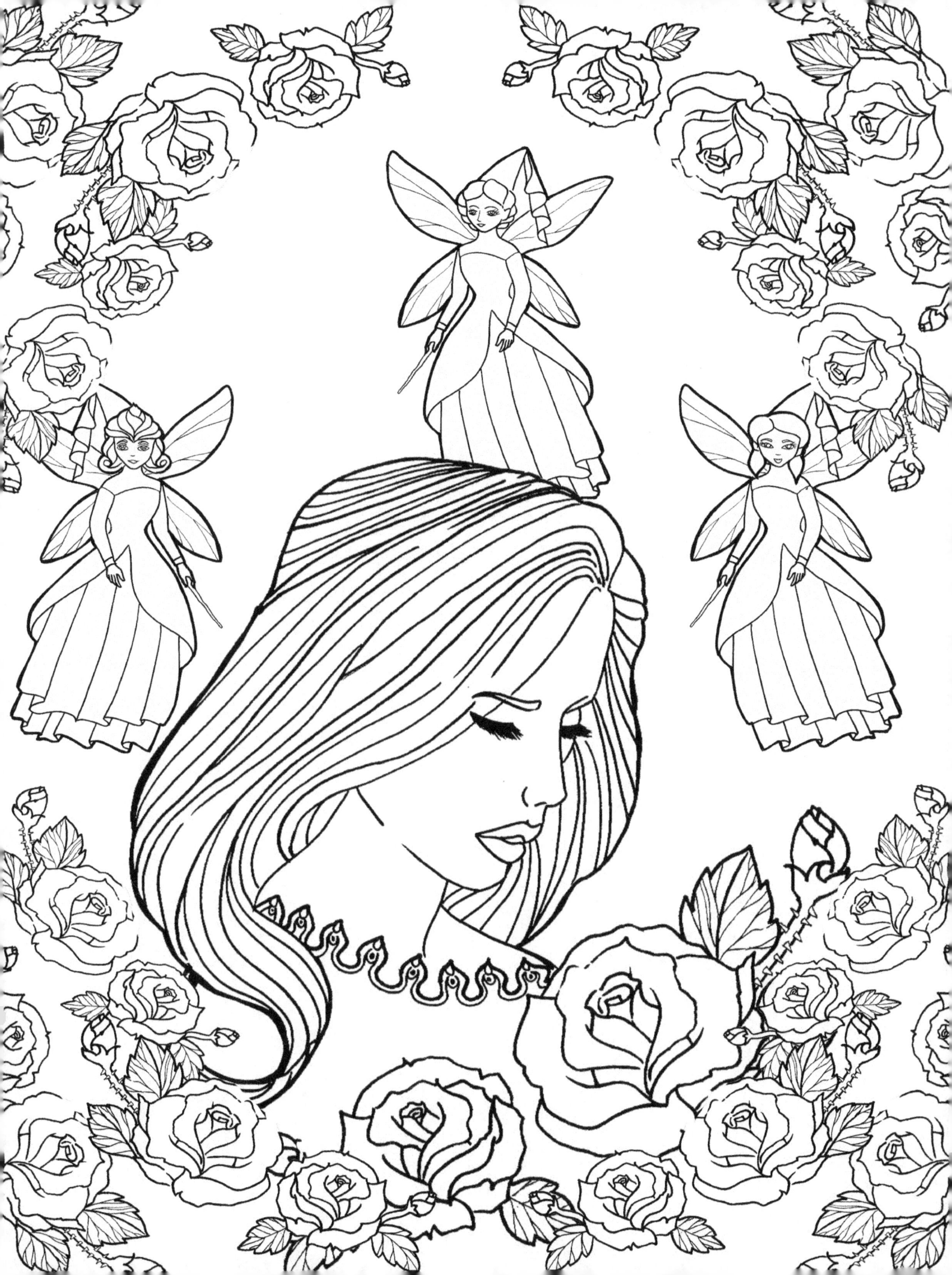

Snow White

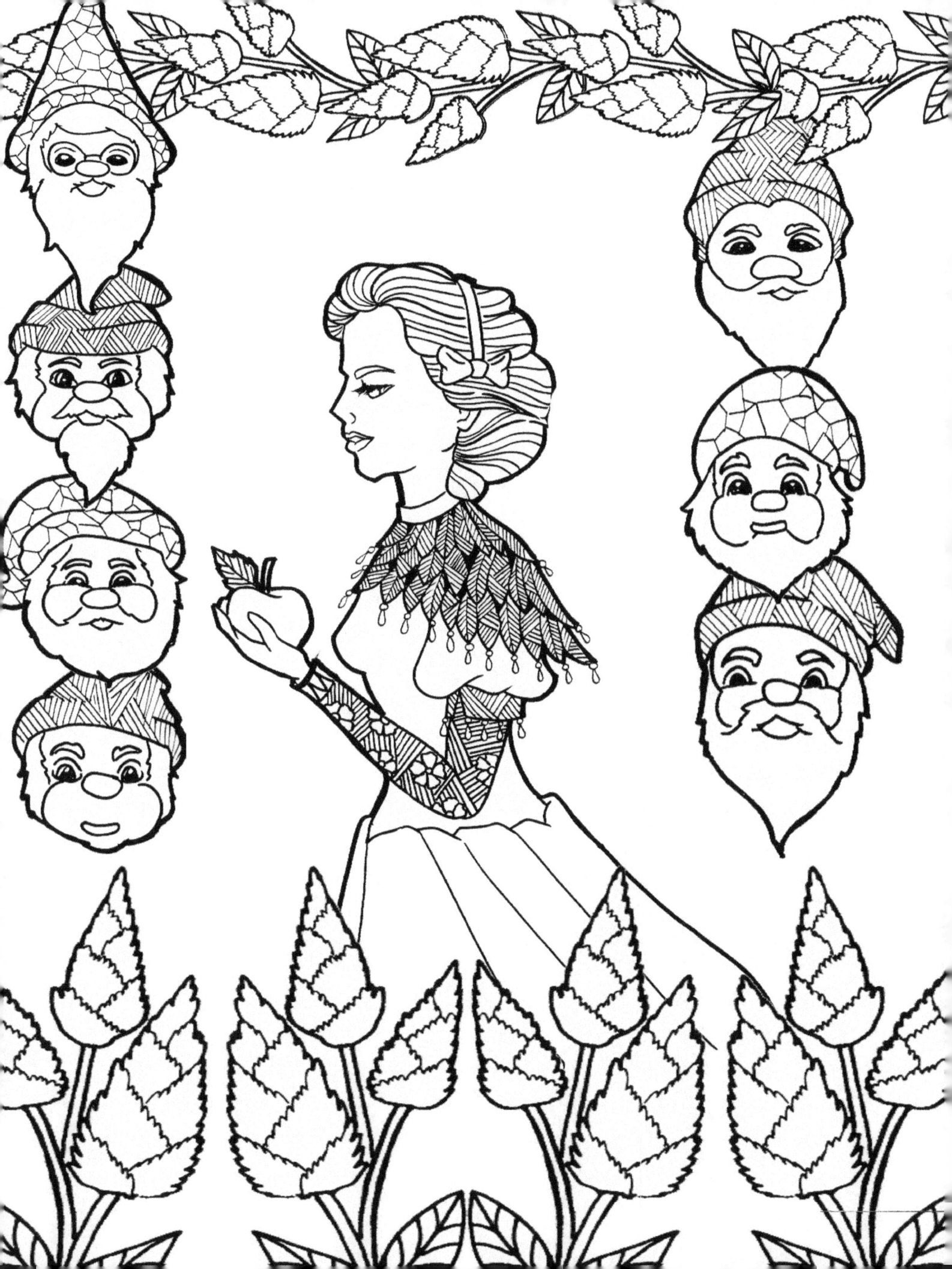

Rumpelstiltskin

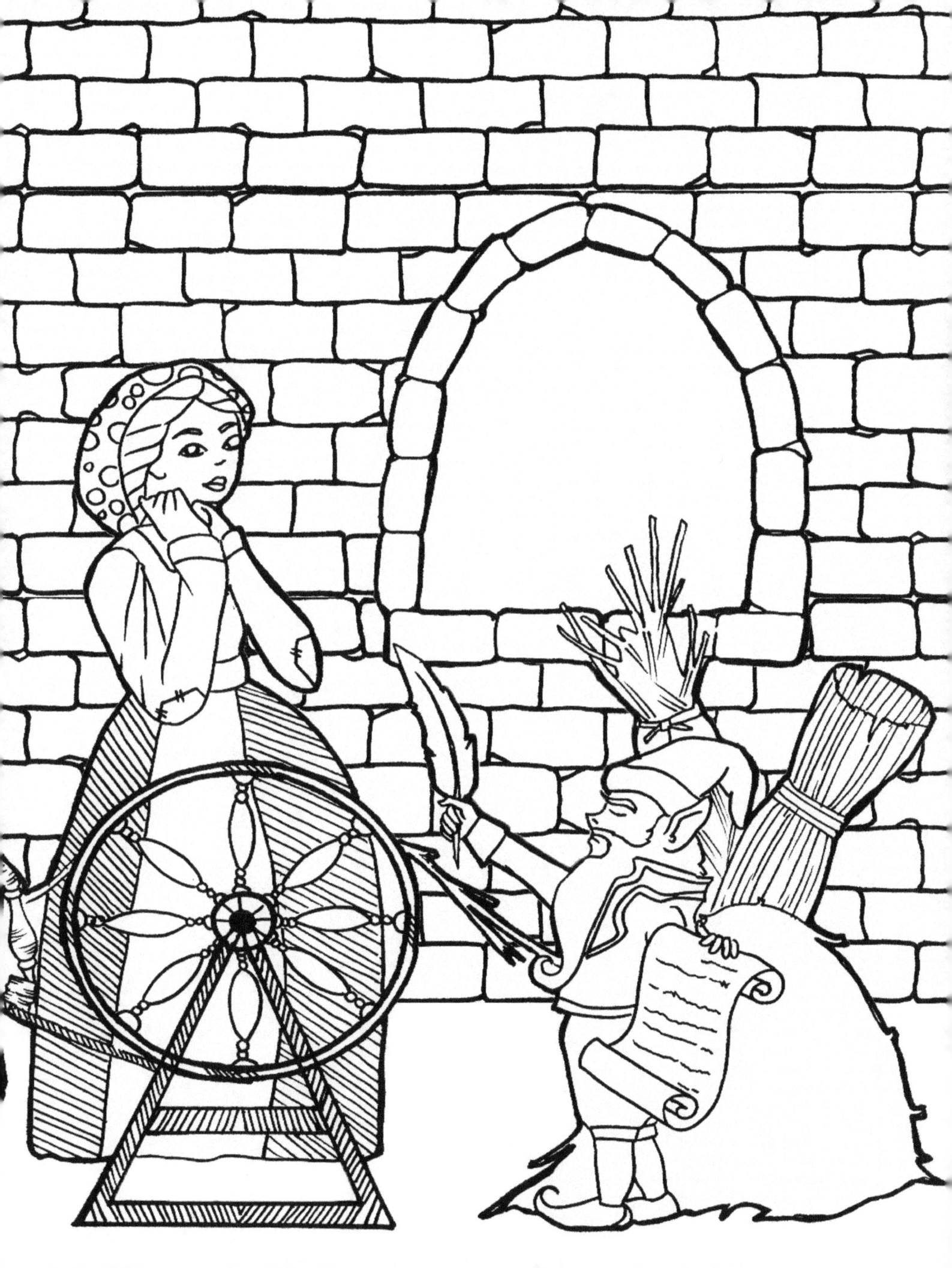

The Queen Bee

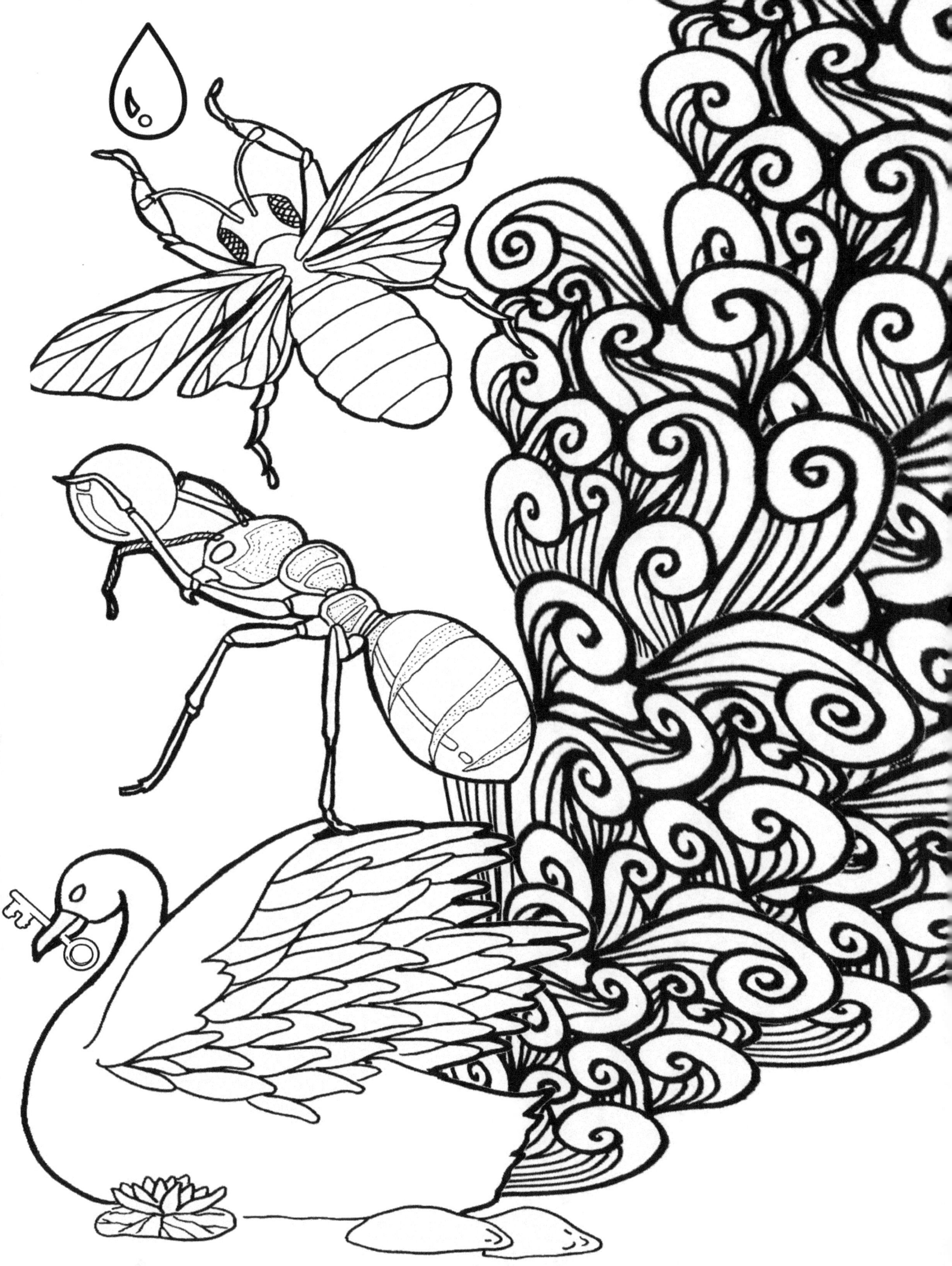

The Wedding
of Mrs. Fox

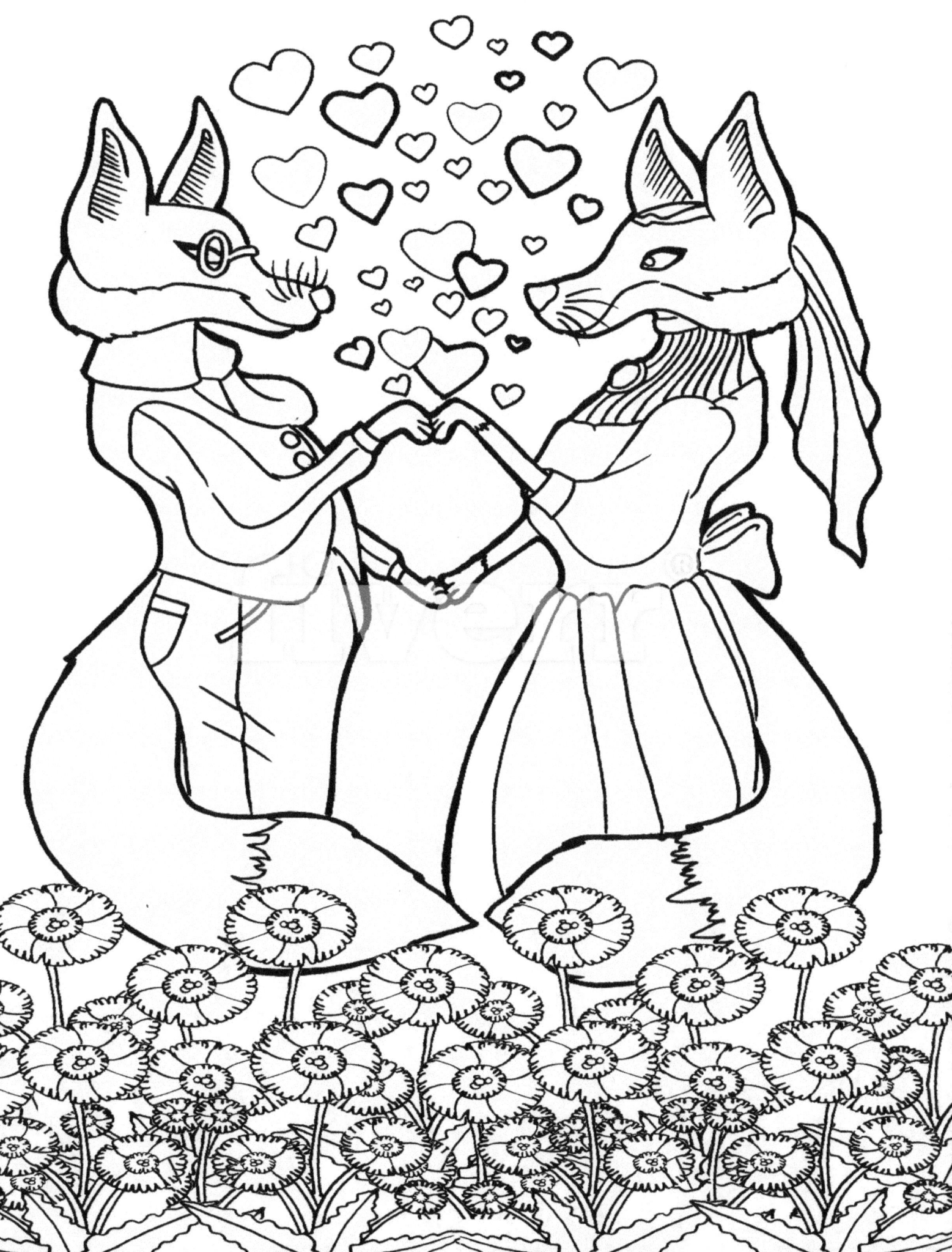

The Three Spinners

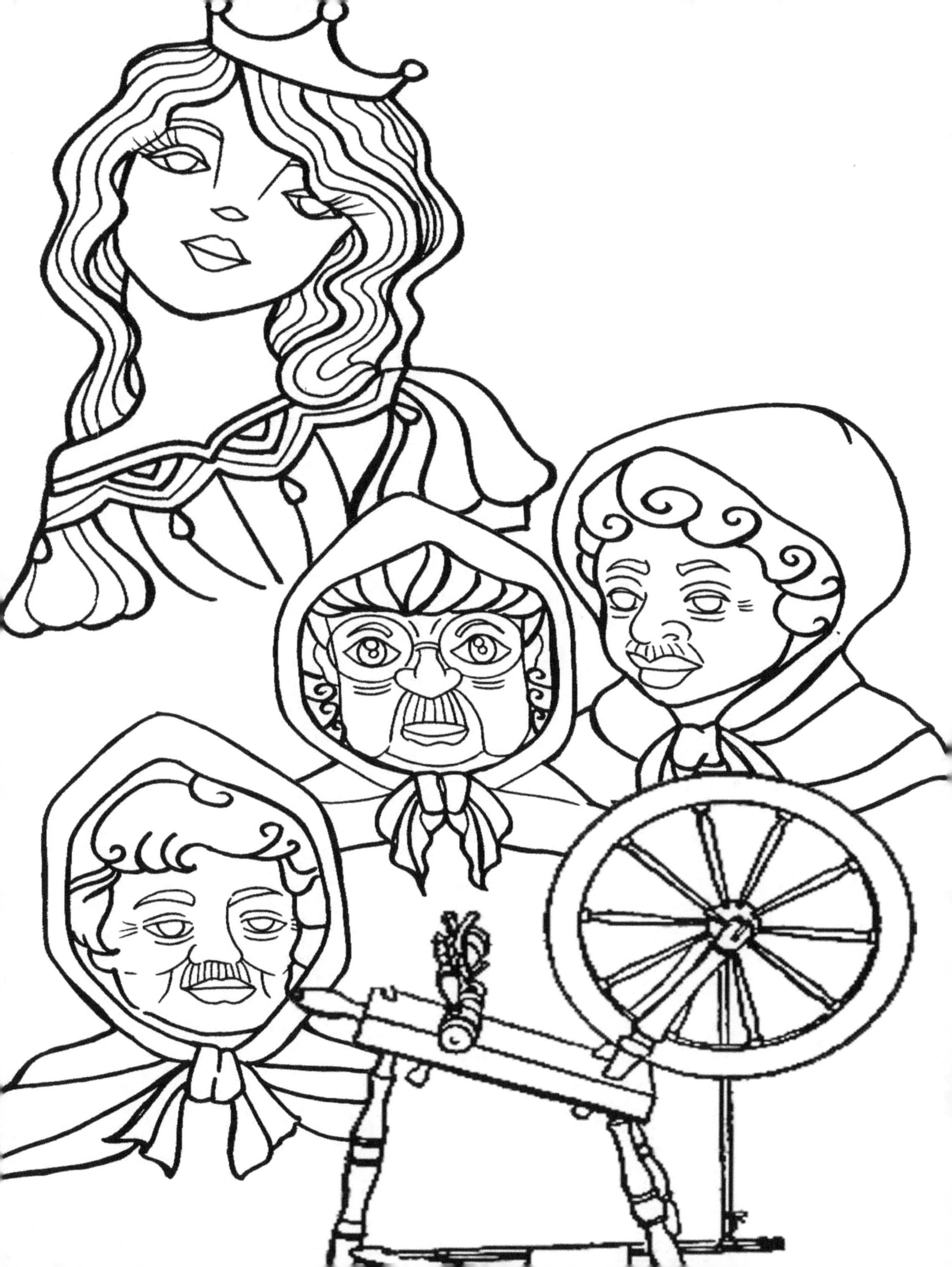

The Tailor

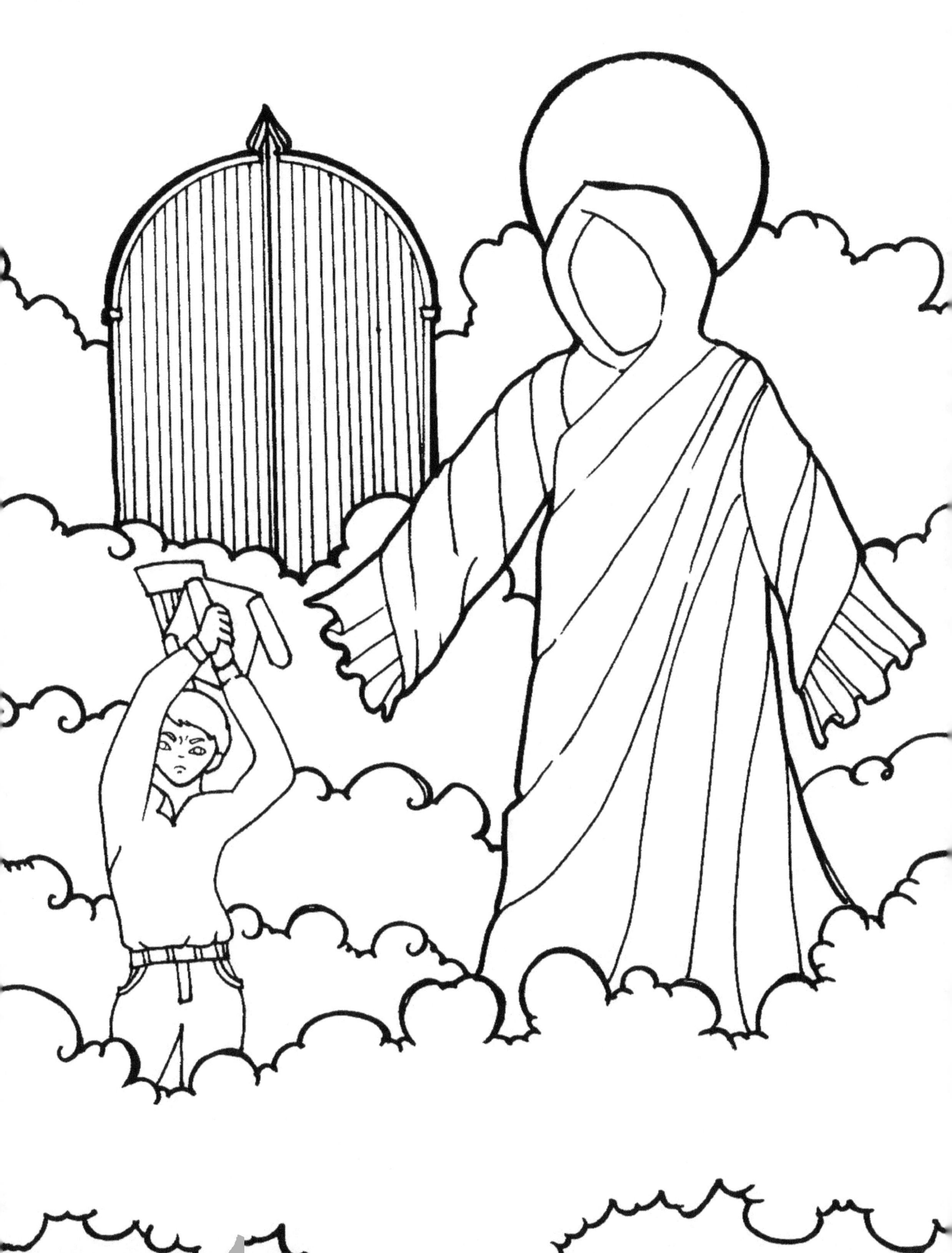

The White Snake

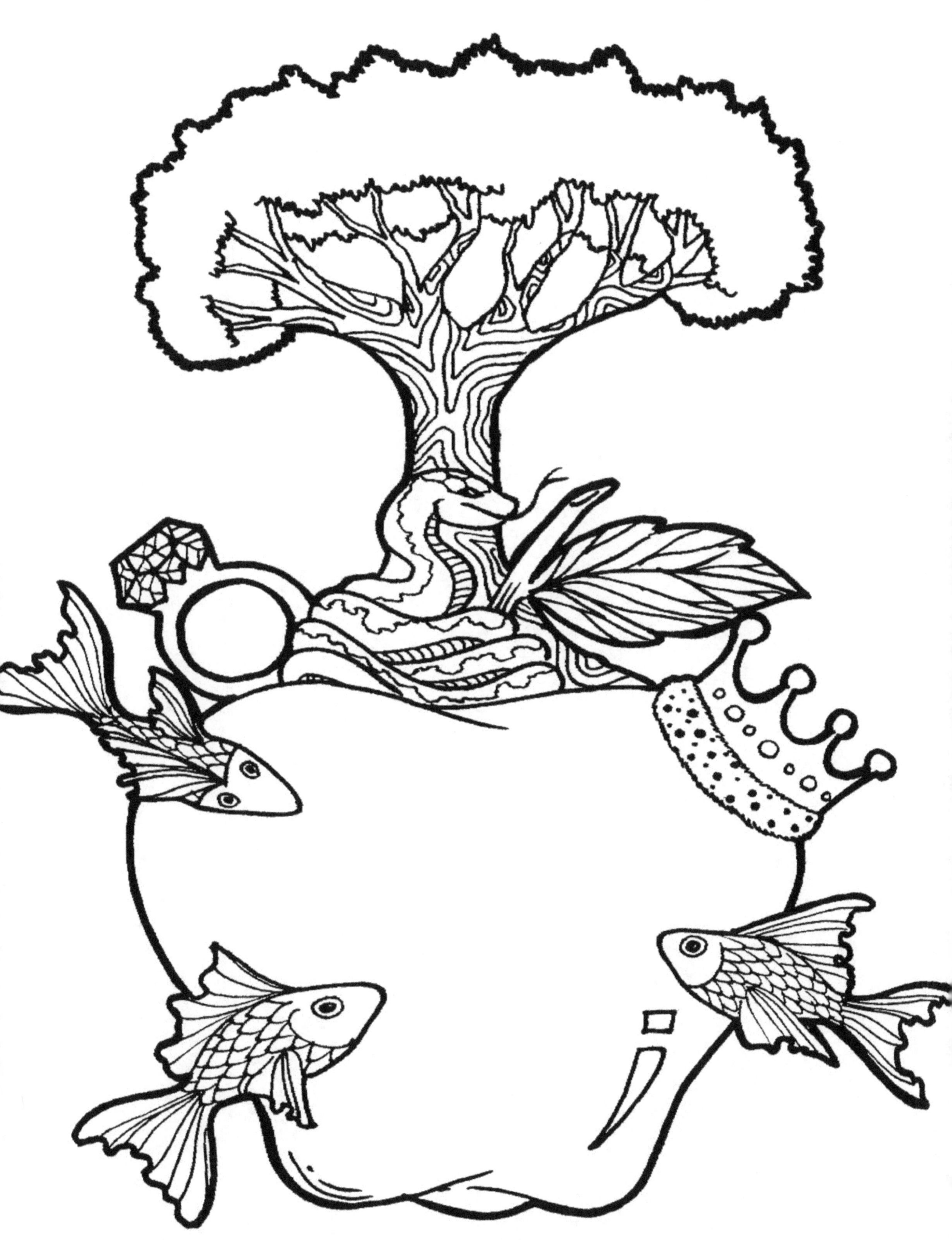

The Three Little Men

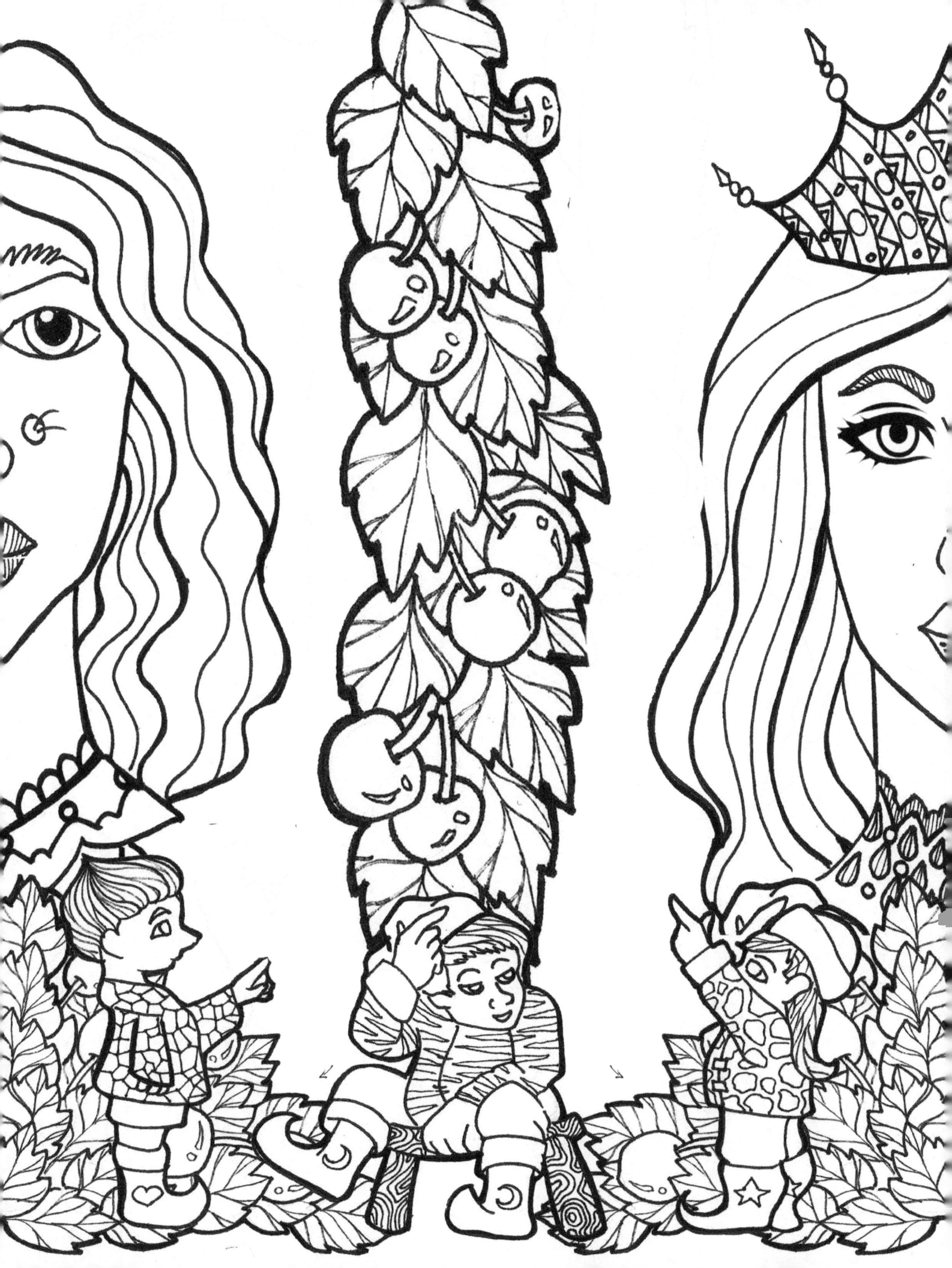

The Juniper Tree

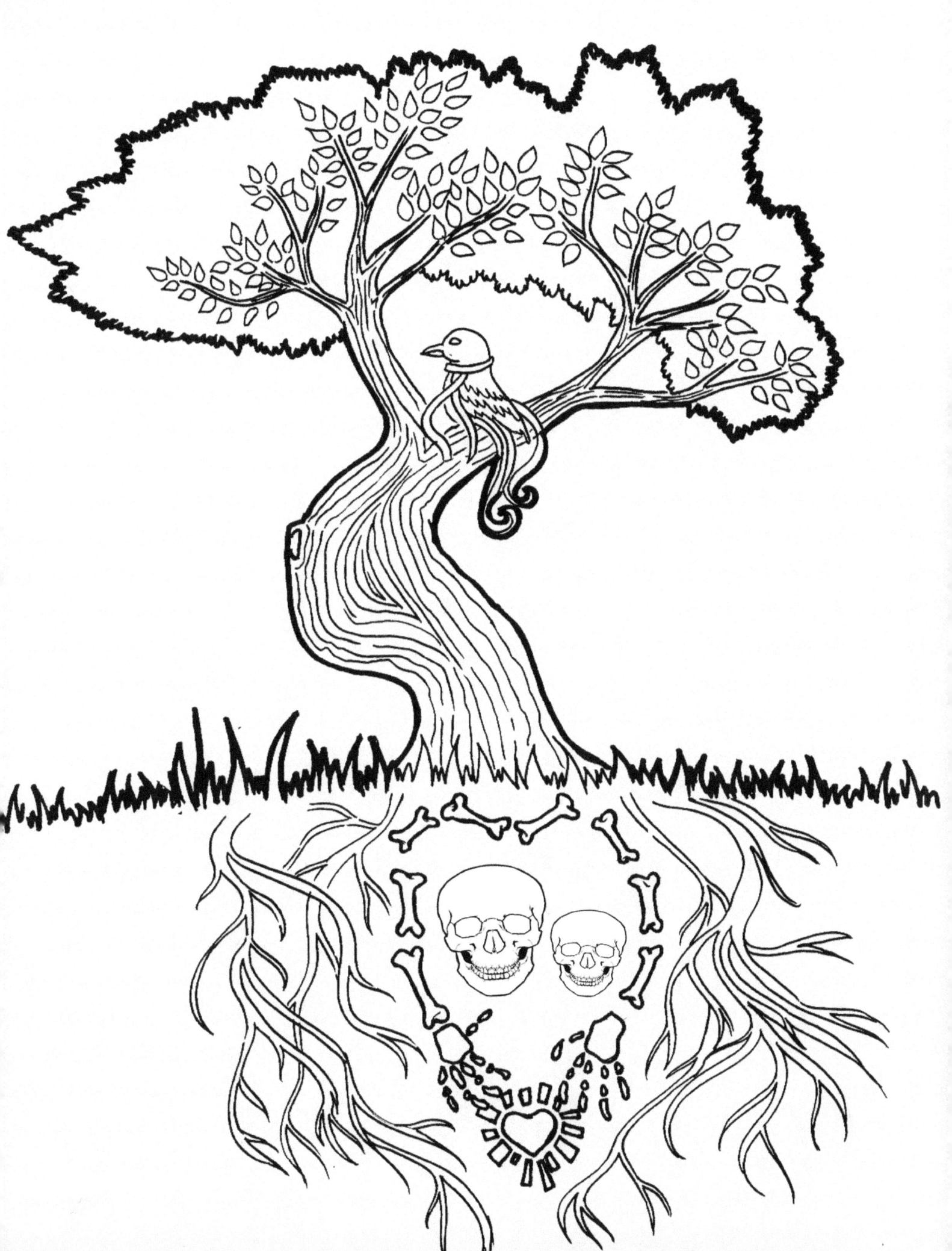

The Golden Bird

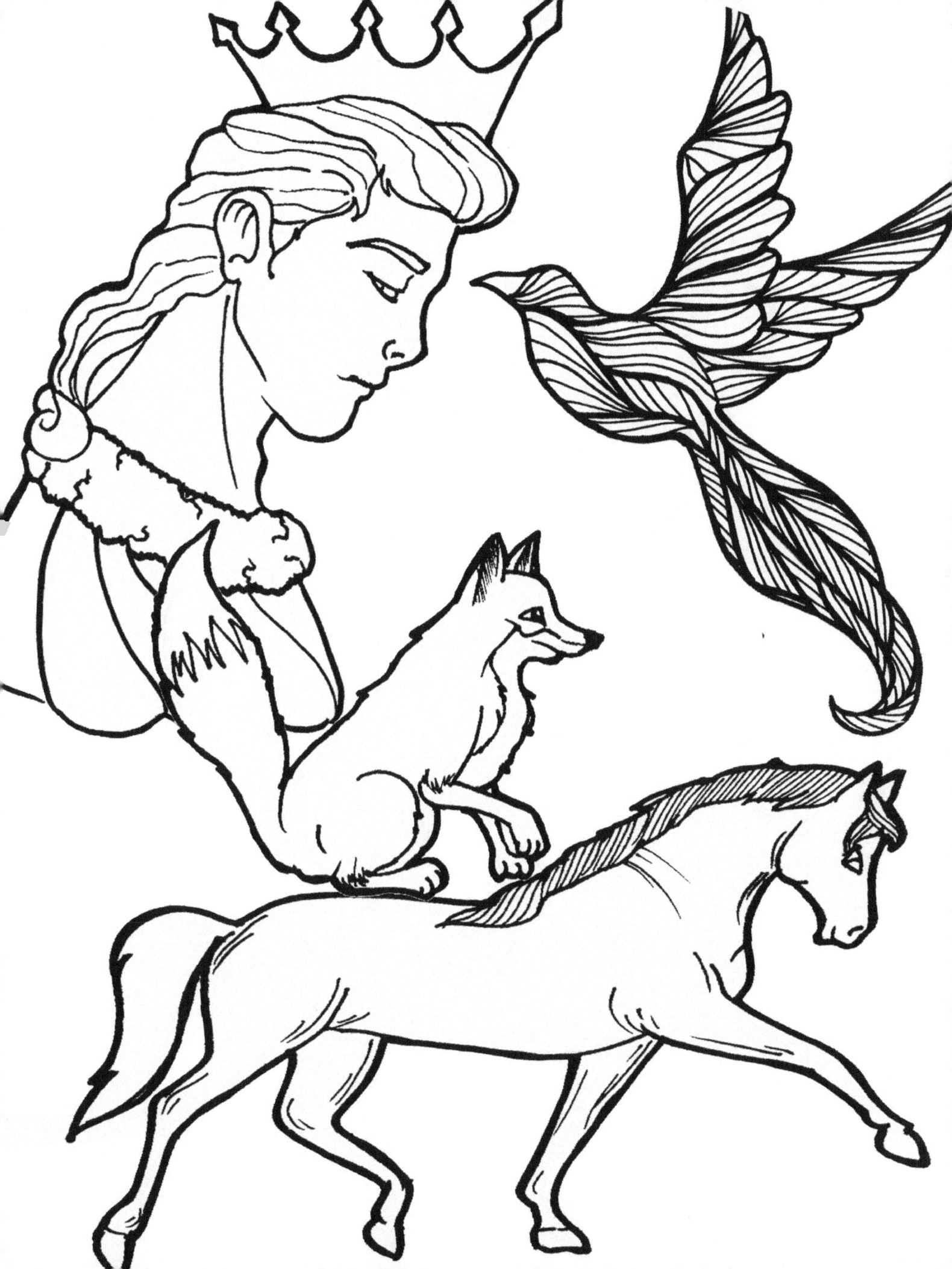

The Golden Goose

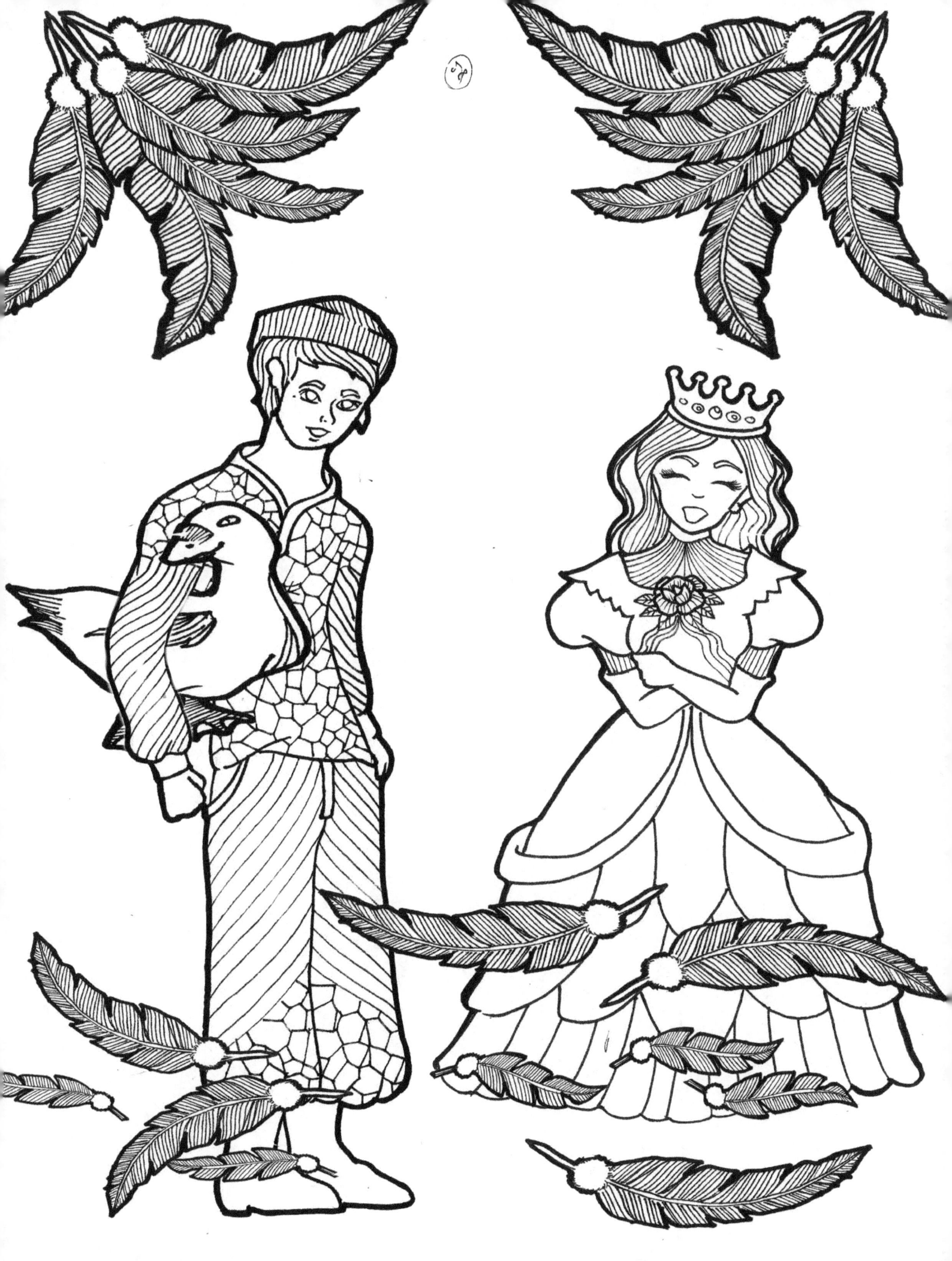

The Twelve Huntsmen

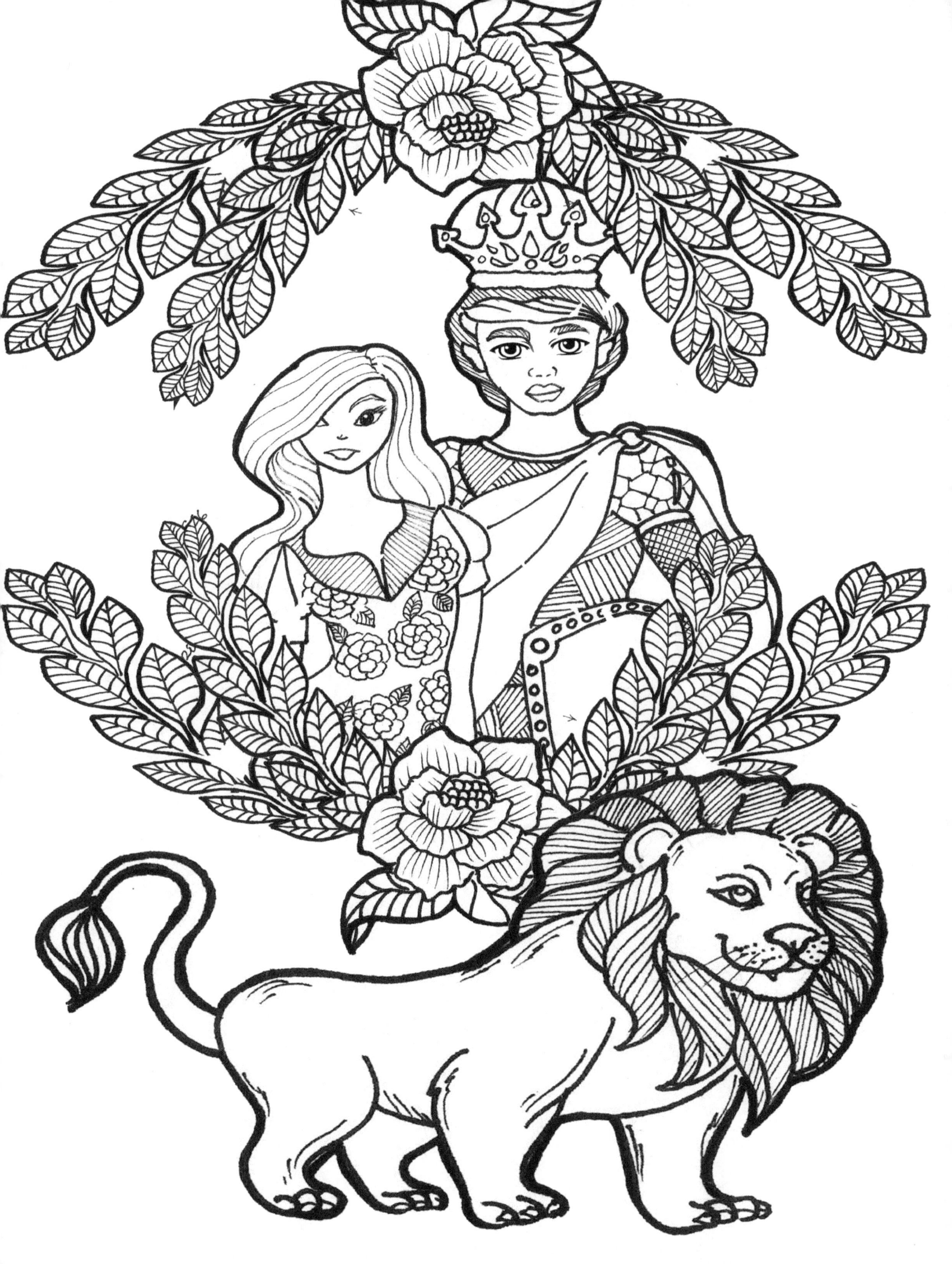

More in the Adult Coloring Book series...

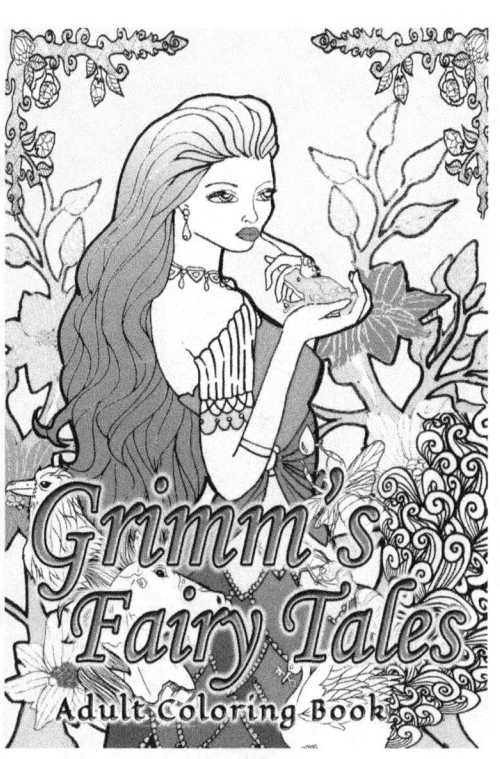

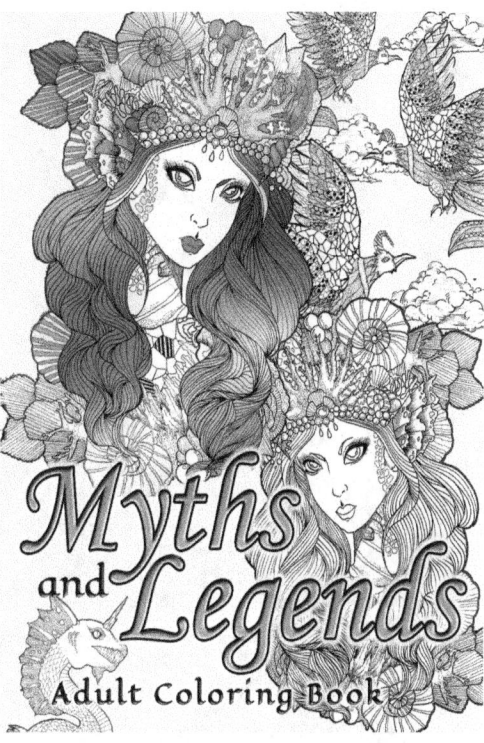

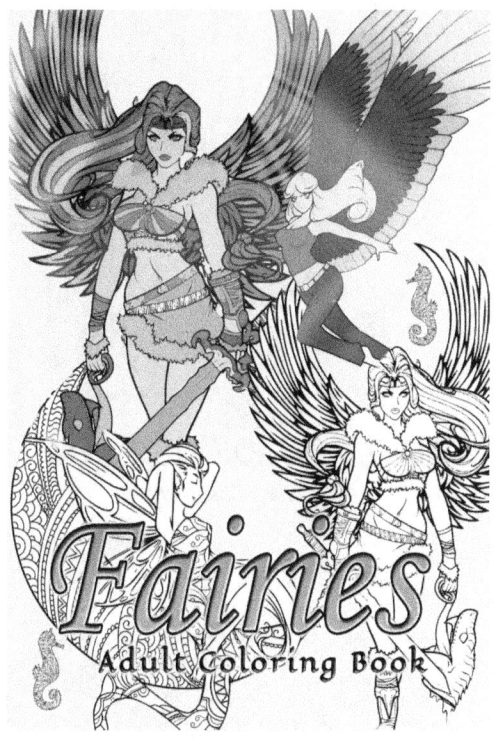

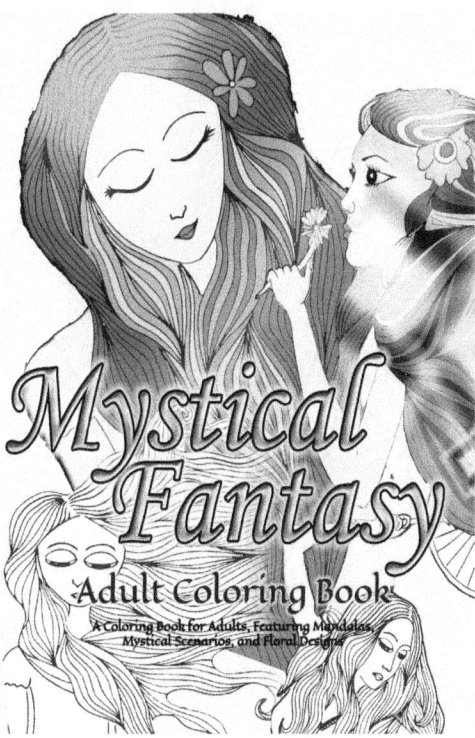

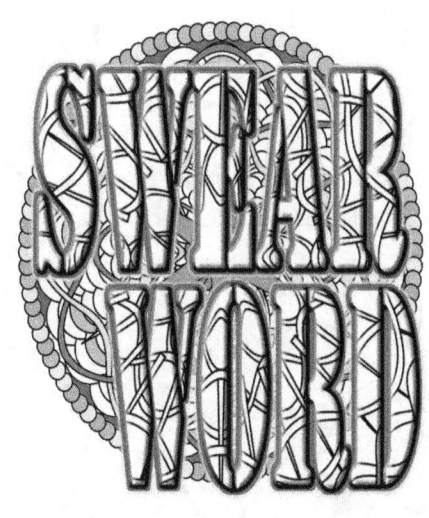

ADULT COLORING BOOK

RELAX WITH CURSE WORDS

ADULT COLORING BOOK

RELAX WITH CURSE WORDS

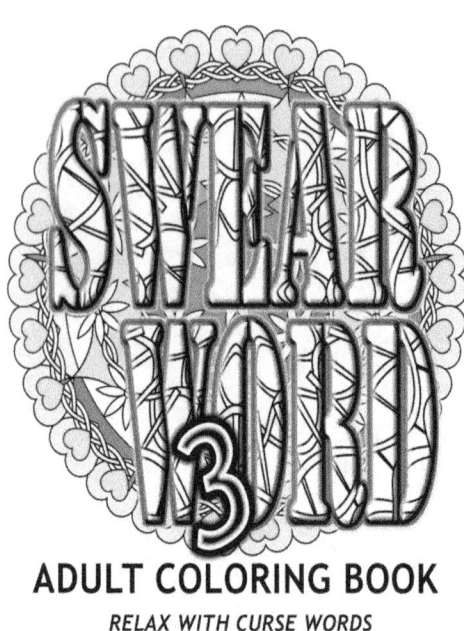

SWEAR WORD 3

ADULT COLORING BOOK

RELAX WITH CURSE WORDS

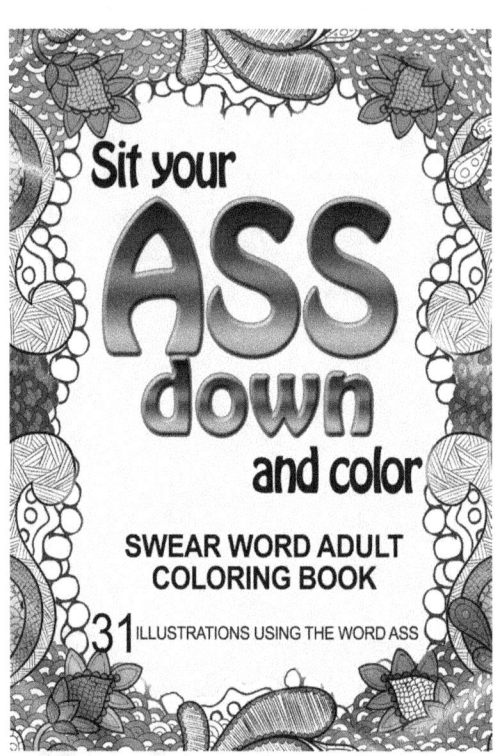

Sit your
ASS
down
and color

**SWEAR WORD ADULT
COLORING BOOK**

31 ILLUSTRATIONS USING THE WORD ASS

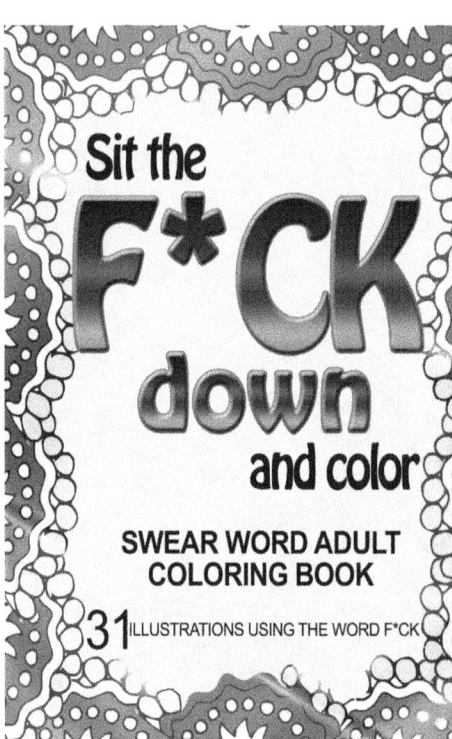

Sit the
F*CK
down
and color

**SWEAR WORD ADULT
COLORING BOOK**

31 ILLUSTRATIONS USING THE WORD F*CK

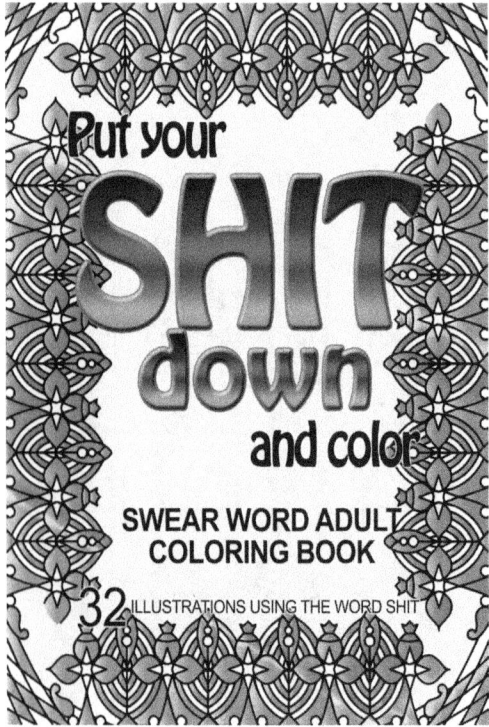

Put your
SHIT
down
and color

**SWEAR WORD ADULT
COLORING BOOK**

32 ILLUSTRATIONS USING THE WORD SHIT

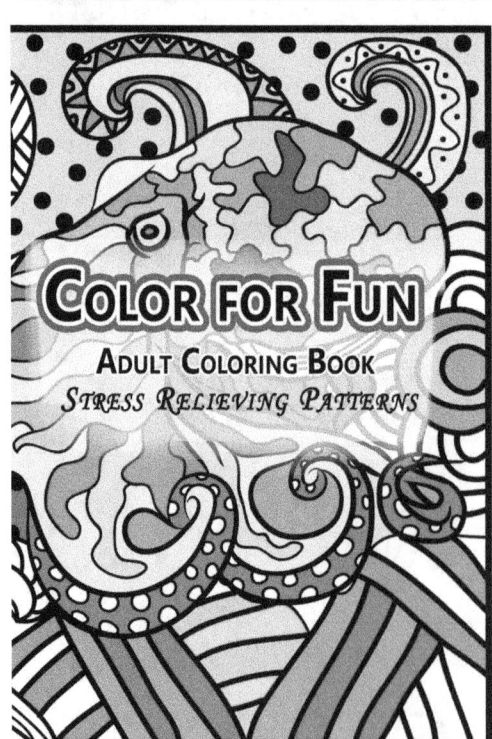

COLOR FOR FUN
ADULT COLORING BOOK
STRESS RELIEVING PATTERNS

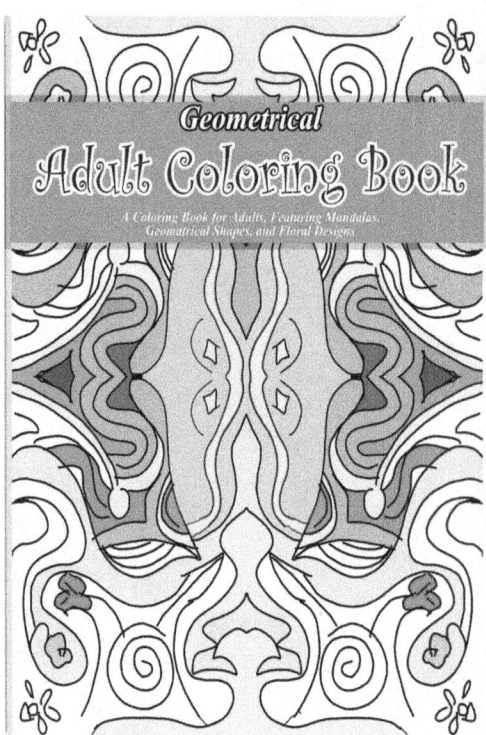

Geometrical
Adult Coloring Book
*A Coloring Book for Adults, Featuring Mandalas,
Geometrical Shapes, and Floral Designs*

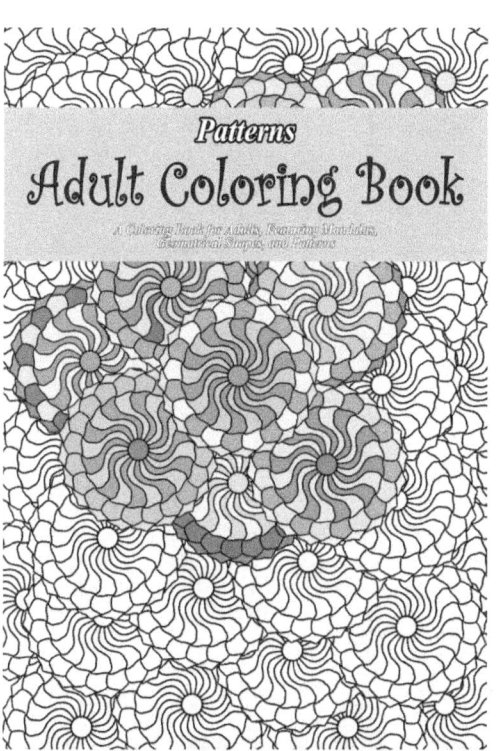

Patterns
Adult Coloring Book

A Coloring Book for Adults, Featuring Mandalas, Geometrical Shapes, and Patterns

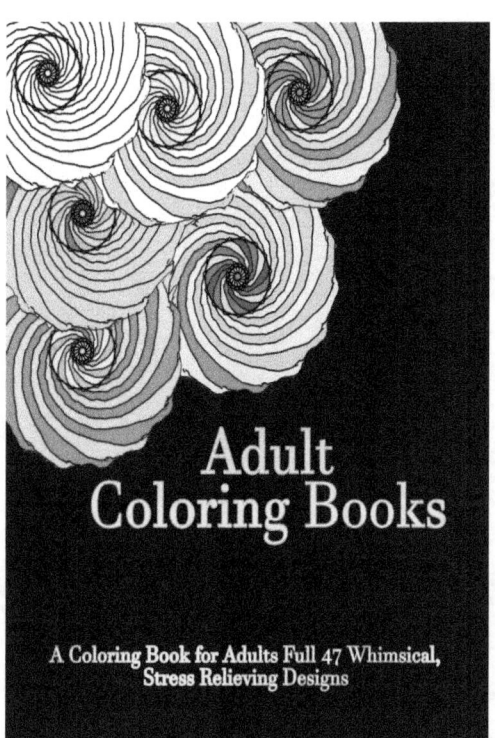

Adult Coloring Books

A Coloring Book for Adults Full 47 Whimsical, Stress Relieving Designs

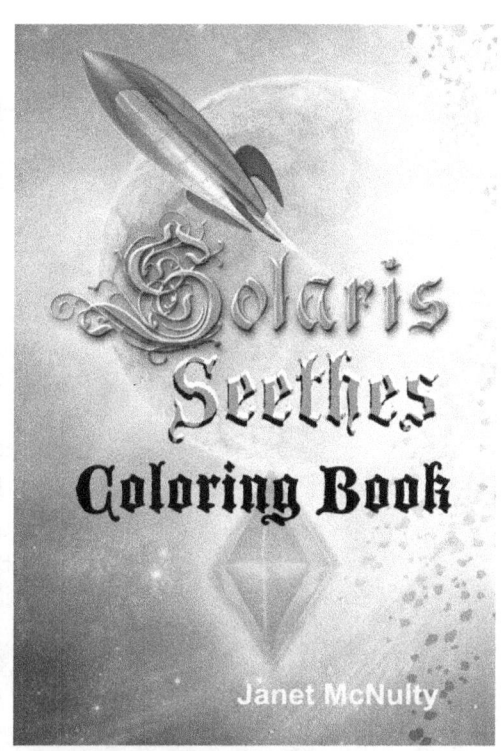

Solaris Seethes
Coloring Book

Janet McNulty

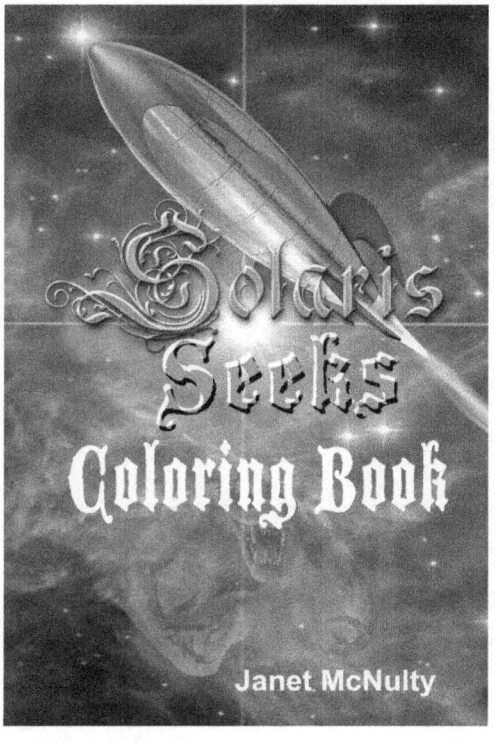

Solaris Seeks
Coloring Book

Janet McNulty

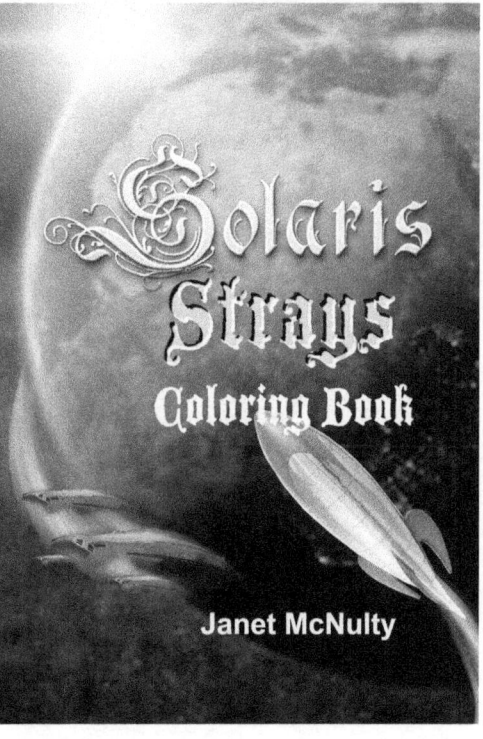

Solaris Strays
Coloring Book

Janet McNulty

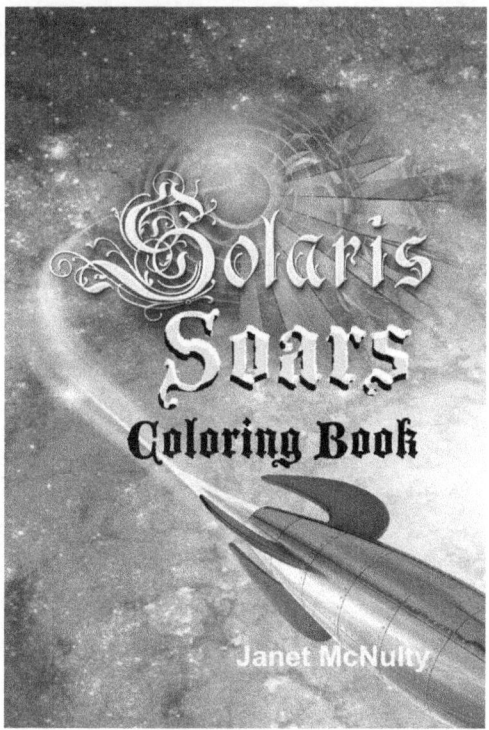

Solaris Soars
Coloring Book

Janet McNulty

www.ingramcontent.com/pod-product-compliance
Lightning Source LLC
Chambersburg PA
CBHW080700190526
45169CB00006B/2195